I0623656

As followers of Christ, there's no escaping the adversity awaiting each of us. Yet many are not armed for the battle ahead of them. In *Take Heed, Watch & Pray*, my friend Lee Cummings provides a training manual that will equip you to overcome the attacks of the enemy so you can endure to the end.

John Bevere
Bestselling Author and Minister
Co-founder, Messenger International & MessengerX

Lee Cummings has a passionate commitment to the intelligent teaching of Scripture and to the moving of the Holy Spirit, which is a rare mixture in our times. For this reason, among others, I believe God has chosen to use Lee's voice to speak to a generation that's longing for an authentic move of God. In his book *Take Heed, Watch & Pray*, Lee clearly lays out the argument that God is looking for a generation that refuses to bend to the spirit of the age or to fall under a spirit of spiritual slumber. Indeed, Lee very clearly points out that we are living in a time when we must be spiritually awakened and engaged to tear down the altars of Baal and to restore the holy altar of the Lord in the Church. *Take Heed, Watch & Pray* will serve as a wake-up call for many, and those with hungry hearts will devour this well-written book.

Rick Renner
Minister, Author, Broadcaster
Moscow, Russia

In these turbulent times, Lee Cummings has written an extremely timely and crucial book for the Church. With deep biblical insight and prophetic urgency, Lee calls every believer to wake up, pay attention, and prepare our hearts for the return of Jesus. This powerful work is a must-read guide to overcoming spiritual deception and walking in intimacy with God amid the chaos of the last days. I highly recommend it!

Jimmy Evans
Founder and President, XO Marriage

A much-needed manual for the last days. Lee Cummings is a leader with both insight and integrity. This book is a well-balanced guide to some of the most critical theological and pastoral matters not only of the days ahead, but the days we are living in right now.

Joel Richardson
Author, *Islamic Antichrist* and *Sinai to Zion*

Lee Cummings is like a "voice crying out in the wilderness," preparing the way for the Lord's return. With the passion of a prophet and the pen of a scholar, Lee has given us a blueprint for living in these last days. Rejecting the fatalism of too many who characterize the Church as weak and ineffective in the last days, this book charts a way forward for an overcoming Church.

Brian Kim
Lead Pastor, HOUSE Denver Colorado

Is your internal life prepared to handle external pressures? It's this question Jesus sought to prepare His disciples for in His last public message. After spending thirty verses describing in detail the birth pangs leading up to His return, Jesus told us how to prepare. He told us to guard our hearts and cultivate a life of prayer and faith in the Word. In *Take Heed, Watch & Pray*, Lee Cummings gives a prophetic call to the Church to focus on the inward realities that will be able to navigate increasing pressure and glory. I cannot say enough about this man and what he means to me and the gift that he is to the global Body of Christ. Get this book!

Corey Russell

Author, *Teach Us to Pray*

Lee Cummings is a wartime pastor. His voice has brought needed clarity and direction to the challenges facing the Church in America. Jesus warned us of the culture wars currently surrounding us. That warning was clear, concise, and direct: Don't be deceived. This book is a battle plan for leaders, parents, and disciples of Jesus Christ. The truths penned on these pages will provide light and needed direction for us. We are not called to simply endure the existing complexities, but to engage them in spirit and truth. Thank you, Lee, for your voice, wisdom, and much-needed leadership.

Michael Miller

UPPERROOM Dallas, Founder and Lead Pastor

Author, *His House, His Presence*

The tragic reality of the day in which we are living is that the casualty rate continues to rise as our adversary continues to seek those he can devour. In this manuscript, Lee Cummings does a masterful job of providing us with a biblical strategy to resist the enemy, while at the same time strengthening those who truly desire to follow in the footsteps of their King in these last days.

Scott Volk
Founder, Together For Israel

Lee Cummings is a courageous leader in the Body of Christ who does not mince words. His fatherly passion to see the Church equipped for the spiritual war waging in the nations is both inspiring and contagious. The book you now hold in your hands serves as a powerful battle plan and strategy to wreak havoc on the enemy's camp. Get your highlighter out and heart ready to pray. The earth has been groaning for a manuscript like this one for a long time. Thank God for our brother Lee who has gifted this generation with this precious treasure. The need has never been greater!

Jeremiah Johnson
Founder, The Altar Global

TAKE HEED WATCH & PRAY

LEE CUMMINGS

Copyright © 2024 by Lee M. Cummings

Radiant Church
8157 E De Avenue
Richland, MI 49083

This book or parts thereof may not be reproduced in any form, stored in a retrieval system, or transmitted in any form by any means—electronic, mechanical, photocopy, recording, or otherwise—without prior written permission of the publisher, except as provided by United States of America copyright law. All rights reserved.

Unless indicated otherwise, Scripture quotations are from the ESV® Bible (The Holy Bible, English Standard Version®), copyright © 2001 by Crossway, a publishing ministry of Good News Publishers. Used by permission. All rights reserved.

Scripture quotations marked (NASB) are taken from the (NASB®) New American Standard Bible®, Copyright © 1960, 1971, 1977, 1995, 2020 by The Lockman Foundation. Used by permission. All rights reserved. lockman.org

Scripture quotations marked (NKJV) are taken from the New King James Version®. Copyright © 1982 by Thomas Nelson. Used by permission. All rights reserved.

Scripture quotations marked (NLT) are taken from the Holy Bible, New Living Translation, copyright ©1996, 2004, 2015 by Tyndale House Foundation. Used by permission of Tyndale House Publishers, Carol Stream, Illinois 60188. All rights reserved.

Scripture quotations marked (KJV) are taken from the King James Version, public domain.

Italics used in Scripture quotations have been added by the author for emphasis.

While the author has made every effort to provide accurate internet addresses at the time of the publication, neither the publisher nor the author assumes any responsibility for errors or for changes that occur after publication.

ISBN: 979-8-9884196-3-1 (paperback)

ISBN: 979-8-9884196-7-9 (e-book)

I dedicate this book to all the courageous pastors of the Radiant Network who are leading God's people during these turbulent times. Your faithfulness to teach the Word of God and call the Church to boldly "arise and shine" is inspiring to me. I am grateful for each one of you and honored to be called your leader.

CONTENTS

ONE
READY TO DEPLOY, ENGAGE &
ENFORCE

THE CHRISTIAN LIFE is not *like* a battle. It *is* a battle. In fact, it is a war zone with a very real, present, and active enemy. He prowls around, looking for those he can take down, take hostage, or take out.[1] And in these days of acceleration, where everything is ramping up toward the end of the age and the return of the Lord Jesus, the spiritual warfare we are experiencing from our adversary the devil is escalating. Unfortunately, it is only going to increase until our Lord comes again.

There is good news, however. The devil has limited authority and power. Jesus, through His death, resurrection, and ascension, destroyed "the works of the devil," "disarmed principalities and powers," conquered death and the grave, and "led captivity captive."[2]

Jesus secured our victory for us against our enemy! Our job is to stand ready to deploy, engage in battle, and enforce Jesus' victory. This means we live in that victory. We walk in that victory. We "put on the whole armor of God" so that we can "stand against the schemes of the devil."[3] We "fight the good fight of the faith."[4] And soon, Jesus, our conquering King, will return, and the devil's defeat will be complete. Until then, we live in the tension of the "in-between"—of the "already but not yet." We live in what C. S. Lewis called "enemy-occupied territory."[5]

ENEMY-OCCUPIED TERRITORY

You see, when Jesus came the first time, He inaugurated God's Kingdom on earth. As Lewis wrote, "The rightful king . . . landed."[6] But when He comes back, His Kingdom will be fully manifested on the earth. In the meantime, we're supposed to do what Jesus taught His disciples to do—*to "occupy" until He comes.*[7] We're to occupy in the occupied zone.

I'm reminded of the last several months of World War 2. As part of a last-ditch effort that would eventually win the war for the Allies, the Allied leadership orchestrated a top secret operation called Operation Overlord, the codename for the Battle of Normandy. Under the cover of darkness, they would launch an airborne and amphibious assault on the beaches of Normandy on what would become known as D-Day and later result in "the successful liberation of German-occupied Western Europe."[8]

On June 6, 1944, over 150,000 Allied troops landed on Normandy beaches. Over 18,000 of them were paratroopers, "dropped into the invasion area to provide tactical support for infantry divisions."[9] These troops engaged in some of the most intense battles over the next eleven months as they continued to drive deeper into the Axis-occupied zone.

A second invasion was launched "from the Mediterranean Sea of southern France (code-named Operation Dragoon)" in

August of 1944, which liberated Paris.[10] Eventually, the Allies' continued push concluded on May 8, 1945. This day, Victory in Europe Day (VE-Day), marked "the formal acceptance by the Allies of . . . Germany's unconditional surrender of its armed forces."[11] The victory that the Allies and the world celebrated in May of 1945 was won tactically in June of the previous year.

ALL THINGS UNDER OUR FEET

Beloved, it is as if we're living in a similar eleven-month period —a time between the D-Day of Jesus' inauguration of His Kingdom on earth and the VE-Day (Victory on Earth Day) of His return and the full establishment of His Kingdom. Like the Allies of World War 2, the Church must fight from a position of victory. *Tactically, the war has already been won.* That's the kind of mentality we must have in these last "in-between" days before Jesus comes again. It is the mentality shift that we need to have in the Body of Christ.

On the one hand, we must know, for example, that the enemy we face is real. Demons are real in this occupied territory. Spiritual warfare is real. The kingdom of darkness is real. But it has been disarmed! And it has been put under our feet. The psalmist David said,

What is man that You are mindful of him, and the son of man that You visit him? For You have made him a little lower than the angels, and You have crowned him with glory and honor. You have made him to have dominion over the works of Your hands; *You have put all things under his feet.*

PSALM 8:4–6 NKJV

The writer of Hebrews further clarified David's words for us when he wrote, "For in that He put all in subjection under him, He left nothing that is not put under him. But now we do not yet see all things put under him. But we see Jesus."[12] Simply because we don't *see* all things under our feet today, they are, nonetheless. And on "the great and magnificent day" of the Lord, on His day of victory, Jesus will split the eastern sky and ride upon the clouds—"and every eye will see him."[13] We will see Him! So, we don't have to fear the devil and his schemes, but we do need to be aware of them and ready to resist them.

Jesus' first coming was D-Day, an invasion behind occupied enemy lines, but VE-Day is only around the corner. Heaven will execute a full-on counteroffensive as Jesus comes and makes all His enemies His "footstool."[14] He will reclaim what He won at the cross, but for now, you and I are still fighting battles in the midst of waiting for His soon return.

So, yes, we live in the war zone in this "present evil age," but we're not fueled by this present age.[15] We're fueled by the age to come—the Kingdom of God. *You may not know it, dear saint, but you are from the future.* You are a citizen of the Kingdom of God that is "already but not yet." The power of the One "who is and who was and who is to come, the Almighty," is within you because He dwells within you by His Holy Spirit.[16] And as John the beloved said, "He who is in you is greater than he who is in the world."[17] Christ in you is greater than the devil and his fellow occupiers.

SATAN'S STRATEGIC PLAN

You must know, however, that the devil has a strategic plan for these last days. It includes an ancient stealth weapon specifically manufactured to be used against the image-bearers of God. It is called deception. *Deception will be deployed as an end-time nuclear weapon.* Just because it has been around for a very long time, don't think it is any less effective. It is still difficult to detect by conventional Christian radar.

All the way back to the very beginning in the garden of Eden, the subtle serpent used deception to detonate rebellion, sin, decay, and death, the ashes of which are still smoldering today. Jesus called Satan "a liar and the father of lies."[18] Satan, then, is the principal engineer, the chief programmer, of deception. And it continues to be his number-one, go-to weapon of mass destruction.

In the Olivet Discourse, Jesus warned His disciples about the deception that would be launched at the end of the age.[19] He said, "See that no one leads you astray. For many will come in my name, saying, 'I am the Christ,' and they will lead many astray."[20] As if to fully punctuate His concern for the deception that will be released, He said again, "For false christs and false prophets will arise and perform great signs and wonders, so as to lead astray, if possible, even the elect."[21]

The devil will add nuclear fuel to his lies in an attempt to take out those outside and even those within the Church. We are seeing this happen around us today. What we're also seeing is something the apostle Paul wrote about to Timothy, his son in the Faith. Paul said, "But the Spirit explicitly says that in later times some will fall away from the faith, paying attention to deceitful spirits and teachings [doctrines] of demons."[22] We know everything in the Bible is the inspired Word of God. Why would Paul have to say, "the Spirit explicitly says"? He said it because the Holy Spirit wanted to capture our attention that the words to follow were of the upmost importance. "THE SPIRIT EXPLICITLY

SAYS"—all caps—that's how we should read those words so as to understand the strong emphasis Paul placed on the very real threat of succumbing to deception in the last days.

Furthermore, both Jesus and Paul called us to wakefulness. Jesus told the disciples to "stay awake," and Paul told the believers in Rome "to wake from sleep."[23] If we're not awake, if we're not watchful and alert, the enemy will infiltrate us and release deception. Even now, there are those who are leaving the Faith—leaders, who are leaving the Faith! And there are those who are calling what is "evil good and good evil," and those who are false prophets and teachers filling social media with their lies and doctrines of demons.[24] Though the victory is secured in Christ against our enemy—though everything is under our feet—Satan is making an all-out assault against us. We must stay awake! *Wakefulness is watchfulness.*

JESUS' COUNTEROFFENSIVE

When I think of the times we're living in, I often think of the opening sentence to *A Tale of Two Cities* by Charles Dickens:

> It was the best of times, it was the worst of times, it was the age of wisdom, it was the age of foolishness, it was the epoch of belief, it was the epoch of incredulity, it was the season of Light, it was the season of Darkness. . . .[25]

The days in which we are living are some of the most dangerous days naturally and spiritually. As Jesus Himself said in the Olivet Discourse regarding the signs of the end of the age, there will be an increase in natural phenomena like earthquakes, famines, and pestilences, as well as an increase of spiritual violence and

keeper to watch. *Watch* therefore, for you do not know when the master of the house is coming—in evening, at midnight, at the crowing of the rooster, or in the morning—lest, coming suddenly, he find you sleeping. And what I say to you, I say to all: *Watch!*

MARK 13:32–37 NKJV

Here is Jesus' secret strategy for us. *Here is what is essential for the battlefield of the last days: Take heed to yourself, keep watch, and pray.* We need to receive these tactical orders from our highest ranking Officer, the Captain of the hosts. Our Captain is calling us first to self-examination—to see if we're still in the Faith or to ensure we've kept ourselves in the love of God.[28] Jesus forewarned the disciples, "And because lawlessness will be increased, the love of many will grow cold."[29] While there is plenty of covert activity going on outside us, we must pay attention to what is happening inside our hearts. We must ask the Holy Spirit to search our hearts and see if there's anything that needs to be addressed. During these days, we must guard our hearts "with all vigilance."[30]

The next tactic is we must watch. Watching is not simply looking. Watching in this instance is a military term. It is speaking in reference to someone who acts like a guard, watchman, or sentinel at night. Our enemy loves to attack under the cover of darkness. It is an advantage because he's able to move in his troops while we're trying rest or unwind. But Jesus commands us to watch—and pray.

This last command is critical to our standing against the adversary at the end of the age. We must pray. As we continue to watch and encounter the events happening around us, we're either going to be filled with faith or filled with anxiety. *When we pray, not only will prayer serve as an antidote to anxiety and a quickening to our faith, but it can go nuclear against the spirit of the age.*

These days of great instability will create the perfect conditions for an Acts 4-type nuclear explosion, all detonated by a praying Church: "And when they had prayed, the place in which they were gathered together was shaken, and they were all filled with the Holy Spirit and continued to speak the word of God with boldness."[31] Our prayers, like those of the early church, will be heavenly radioactive, clearing the enemy-occupied territory and readying it for our King's return.

Beloved, make no mistake about it, Jesus wanted His disciples to stand ready. He wanted them to have clarity and sobriety. He wanted them to have faith, not fear—to be proactive, not reactive. He wants that for you and me, too. He wants us to live expectantly, prepared for His return. The big question for us is this: Are we ready? I'm not talking about being saved. As Christians, we know and understand there is no entrance into the Kingdom of God—no eternal life—apart from faith in Jesus Christ, the Son of God. What I am talking about is more like being one of those five virgins Jesus drew our attention to in the parable of the ten virgins.[32] I'm meaning the five who, when the master returned, had their lamps trimmed and had sufficient oil. Are you ready like that? Am I?

I don't want to be blindsided by Jesus' return. I don't want to be caught unaware or unprepared. I don't want Him to find me deceived, asleep, or MIA. I don't want that for you, either. *I want us—His Church—to be awake, watchful, wise, and ready.* That's why I wrote this book—to help the Bride make herself ready.[33]

In the pages that follow, we're going to look more closely at what Jesus said would take place at the end of the age. It is important for us to know the signs of His return, what to expect in the coming revival, and how best to calibrate our hearts to the Kingdom of God in readiness for what will take place. We'll take a look at the spirit of the age and what Scripture meant by "as in the days of Noah."[34] We'll see the real battle taking place in the world is the battle of the altar. We'll get a glimpse of the controversies that will be colliding at the end of the age, and the test the Church will have to face. Together, we'll discover how to stay awake and defuse hell's nuclear weapon of deception. Finally, we'll learn how to take heed, watch, and pray so that we overcome in the last days.

---

1. See John 8:44; 2 Timothy 2:26; 1 Peter 5:8; Revelation 2:10.
2. See 1 Corinthians 15:54–56. Ephesians 4:8 (NKJV); Colossians 2:15 (NKJV); 1 John 3:8.
3. Ephesians 6:11.
4. 1 Timothy 6:12.
5. C. S. Lewis, *Mere Christianity,* (New York: HarperOne, 2015), 46.
6. Ibid.
7. Luke 19:13 (KJV).
8. Wikipedia contributors, "Operation Overlord," *Wikipedia,* https://en.wikipedia.org/wiki/Operation_Overlord/ (accessed January 9, 2024).
9. Imperial War Museum, "The 10 Things You Need to Know about D-Day," *IWM,* https://www.iwm.org.uk/history/the-10-things-you-need-to-know-about-d-day/ (accessed January 1, 2024).
10. Ibid.
11. Wikipedia contributors, "Victory in Europe Day," *Wikipedia,* https://w.wiki/3k5M/ (accessed January 9, 2024).
12. Hebrews 2:8–9 (NKJV).
13. Acts 2:20; Revelation 1:7.
14. Psalm 110:1.
15. Galatians 1:4.
16. Revelation 1:8.
17. 1 John 4:4.
18. John 8:44.

19. The Olivet Discourse is found in the synoptic Gospels—Matthew, Mark, and Luke—more specifically, in Matthew 24–25, Mark 13, and Luke 21. Jesus taught His disciples about the signs accompanying His return. The discourse was given on the Mount of Olives.
20. Matthew 24:4–5.
21. Matthew 24:24.
22. 1 Timothy 4:1 NASB.
23. Matthew 24:42–43; Mark 13:34–35, 37; Luke 21:36; Romans 13:11.
24. Isaiah 5:20.
25. Charles Dickens, *A Tale of Two Cities,* (New York: Penguin Books, 2000), 5.
26. Matthew 24:6; Mark 13:7; Luke 21:10–11, 20.
27. Matthew 24:14.
28. See 2 Corinthians 13:5; Jude 1:21.
29. Matthew 24:12.
30. Proverbs 4:23.
31. Acts 4:31.
32. See Matthew 25:1–13.
33. See Revelation 19:7.
34. Matthew 24:37.

TWO
THE OMEGA GENERATION &
END-TIME EVENTS

WE CAN FEEL the pressure created by the current and impending signs. We are experiencing "the beginning of the birth pains" or contractions that Jesus spoke about in Matthew 24:8 and Mark 13:8. But the fact is we've been living in the last days for a long time—since the day of Pentecost in Acts 2.

After the Holy Spirit was poured out on the 120 believers gathered in the Upper Room, the apostle Peter began his sermon by explaining what had happened and what the bystanders had witnessed as a result. Quoting from Joel 2:28, Peter said, "And in the last days it shall be, God declares, that I will pour out my Spirit on all flesh."[1] *The outpouring of the Holy Spirit upon the Church as well as the birth of the Church started the countdown clock for the return of the Lord.*

With a countdown clock, there is a growing sense of urgency. For instance, if you're playing a football or a basketball game, and two minutes remain on the game clock, you get a real sense that time is of the essence. You know you have to focus and complete the go-to plays you've practiced hundreds of times. You also know that, if you don't manage the clock well, you're not going to win.

Everything that God communicated in biblical prophecy is there so that you and I who live at the end of the age will be able to look at the countdown clock and know what time it is, what things are supposed to happen, how we should live, and what we must do. *With the clock running down, we know we cannot afford to live life as usual.* If you haven't realized it yet, by the way, "as usual" and "normal" died around the time COVID mercilessly migrated throughout the world. This and other events demonstrate we are living in unprecedented days.

One generation will see Jesus Christ come again. It will be the last generation—the Omega Generation—living on the earth when He appears. The Omega Generation will not be composed only of one specific age group, race, or ethnicity, per se. It will be a marked population of people living collectively at one time, experiencing the significant events of the end times. I believe we could very well be that generation. And the reason I think we could be living in the last of the last days and be the generation to see the return of the Lord is we have witnessed and are witnessing three prophetic indications that are game changers:

1. The creation of the State of Israel
2. The acceleration of technology
3. The advancement of the gospel

I call these three indicators *game changers* because they have never happened, nor could happen, at any other time in history. Of course, there are other important signs which we'll look at in this chapter, but these three underscore how close the return of our Lord is. He is coming soon.

THE CREATION OF THE STATE OF ISRAEL

On May 14, 1948, Israel became a nation again. "David Ben-Gurion, the head of the Jewish Agency, proclaimed the establishment of the State of Israel. U.S. President Harry S. Truman recognized the new nation on the same day."[2] What was so significant about this?

Nations have come and gone throughout human history. But *Israel is the only nation that ceased to exist and then became a nation again.* And she did this twice. As David Parsons, the vice president and senior spokesman for the International Christian Embassy Jerusalem, has said:

> The fact is that the Jews are the only people who have been thoroughly uprooted from their homeland, only to return to that land and re-establish their national sovereignty. You could search far and wide and still not find another people who have managed to do that once, and yet the Jews have done it twice![3]

The first time Israel returned from exile was after the Babylonian captivity. The second time was after World War 2 in 1948. Having lost her land and independence 2,000 years before —her people having been scattered throughout the world yet keeping and maintaining their Jewish identity—the nation was reborn in a day. The prophet Isaiah said, "Who has heard such a thing? Who has seen such a thing? Shall a land be born in one day? Shall a nation be brought forth in one moment?"[4] Israel was. And that's just how significant her rebirth was for all time, but especially for our time.

Jesus alluded to the re-emergence of the nation of Israel when He taught the lesson of the fig tree. He said, "From the fig tree learn its lesson: as soon as its branch becomes tender and puts out its leaves, you know that summer is near."[5] Often in Scripture, the fig tree was used as a symbol of the nation of Israel.[6] And in the case of the prophetic timetable Jesus was giving His disciples, Jesus was telling them to pay attention to Israel. *Israel was to be their and our timepiece.*

In Luke 21:20–24, Jesus warned of the judgments that were shortly to come to the nation of Israel. Because she rejected her Messiah, disciplinary action would soon come. Jerusalem would be destroyed, and the Jews dispersed among the nations. That destruction and dispersion happened in AD 70. But then, as Jeremiah 29:14 promised, the Lord would bring them back:

> "I will be found by you, declares the Lord, and I will restore your fortunes and gather you from all the nations and all the places where I have driven you, declares the Lord, and I will bring you back to the place from which I sent you into exile."

Only one time in Israel's history was she scattered to the nations, and that was in AD 70. This second return to the land was the one promised prior to Jesus' return or what Jesus called the fulfillment of "the times of the Gentiles."

This was a real game changer. It tells us there is something very significant in the age in which we're living—that no other generation could have pointed to and said, "That's happening in our generation." We don't know the very day or the hour of the second coming, but heaven has put us on notice. The timepiece of Israel is telling us to pay attention.

THE ACCELERATION OF TECHNOLOGY

Technology is a major game changer. Since the late 1800s and the Industrial Revolution until now, we have seen technology advance in leaps and bounds. Man's first flight happened only 120 years ago, telephone "land lines" became widely used by the public about 100 years ago, and the first personal computers were mass-marketed 40 to 50 years ago.[7]

Today, land lines are all but obsolete, you can fly almost anywhere around the world in a matter of hours, and we've gone from personal computers to personal devices. We're now using Artificial Intelligence (AI) to plan meetings, write blogs and books, design component hardware for spaceships, and numerous other things we're discovering it can do with us (or maybe even without us). Then there's the widespread use of quantum computing that will speed up everything and that exponentially!

When we look at biblical prophecies about the end of the age, we discover some of those prophecies can only happen with the advancement of technology. The prophet Daniel, as an example, received a direct revelation from an angel about God's plans for Israel in the last days.[8] At the end of that revelation, the angel said, "But you, Daniel, shut up the word and seal the book, until the time of the end. Many shall run to and fro, and knowledge shall increase."[9] There have been those who have pointed at global travel and asserted this was what the angel was referring to when he said, "Many shall run to and fro." Though that may be a certain application of that verse, most scholars agree that it is meaning people going to and fro for knowledge, desperately searching for answers or wisdom. I believe one of the places people will run to are the Scriptures. As the end of the age draws closer and events are happening around us, we will have a sense of urgency and want to understand what's happening and what we should do.

The angel said another thing that's important for us. He said knowledge would increase. The Hebrew word used for *knowledge* in this verse is the same word used to describe the technical knowledge and understanding that Bezalel needed to build the tabernacle.[10] But even before Bezalel, human technology was used to build the Tower of Babel. They didn't use stones. They made bricks.

> And they said to one another, "Come, let us make bricks, and burn them thoroughly." And they had brick for stone, and bitumen for mortar. Then they said, 'Come, let us build ourselves a city and a tower with its top in the heavens, and let us make a name for ourselves, lest we be dispersed over the face of the whole earth."
>
> GENESIS 11:2–4

Like other builders in other civilizations that came after them, they wanted to build into the heavens and access the place where they believed the gods lived. Wanting to build a name for themselves, wanting to secure the information and secrets of the gods, such civilizations would build artificial mountains or great wonders like the pyramids.

So, what did God do about the Tower of Babel? He confused the language of the people there so that they couldn't understand one another, and He "dispersed them from there."[11] He scattered them.

Now, here's what's mind-blowing. *It has taken some 6,000 years for the human race to undo what God did at the Tower of Babel.* And we've seen it come full circle in our generation! For the first time in human history, we can communicate commonly and freely with almost anyone on the face of the earth without learning another language or culture, or even traveling across the globe. We now have the World Wide Web, cell phones, and personal devices we can use to FaceTime, Zoom, or just speak to anyone who has access to these, and most everyone does. There's even an app you can download on your phone called Babbel. If you talk into it and select what language you want your words to be translated into, the app will do it for you, allowing you a means to communicate to someone in a language they know and understand—a language you aren't fluent in.

Telecommunication and travel have seemingly shrunk the world back to one people with one language, showing us the very real plausibility of the nations coming under a one-world system or order. But the good news about the advancement of technology is how it has become a game changer in these last days to fulfill the Great Commission.

THE ADVANCEMENT OF THE GOSPEL

In Matthew 28:19–20, after His resurrection, Jesus commissioned His disciples:

> Go therefore and make disciples of all nations, baptizing them
> in the name of the Father and of the Son and of the Holy Spirit,

teaching them to observe all that I have commanded you. And behold, I am with you always, to the end of the age.

Since that time, the disciples from every generation have been using many means to propagate the gospel in every land. We've gone as missionaries, we've printed gospel tracts and books, we've communicated by satellite and internet broadcasts, and we've traveled the world over, preaching and teaching.

As of 2024, there are 8 billion people on the globe, and 12,114 people groups—7,250 of those are unreached (4.8 billion people).[12] In 2009, Franklin Graham wrote an article entitled, "The World is Ripe for Harvest." He said, "Only in our generation has it become conceivable that Christians could complete the task of reaching 'every nation, tribe, people and language' (Revelation 7:9, NIV)."[13] Though we Christians have enough money and people to send in missions, and we have the technology and means to reach every unreached people group, we must do the work. Missionary Portal summed it up this way, "We have enough money and people to send missionaries to every unreached people group. But not enough people are giving, and not enough people are going."[14] For the first time in history, however, we can see the possibility of reaching the world for Christ. In fact, we're seeing just how quickly end-time prophecy can become reality in years and even days.

END-TIME SIGNS

Now that we've reviewed the game changers, what else did Jesus say to look for at the end of the age? Well, Jesus used metaphorical language of birth pains or contractions to tell us that, the closer we get to end of the age, the signs that He gave, like contractions, would become more and more frequent, and more and more intense. Many of these signs, then, have appeared in earlier generations. However, one look at current events around the globe, and we see these signs are appearing more frequently and intensifying. This tells us the birth pains are upon us.

Here's a list of what Jesus told us we would see at the end of the age:

- False christs
- Deception
- Wars and rumors of wars
- Nations rising up against other nations
- Kingdoms rising up against other kingdoms
- Famines
- Earthquakes
- Pestilences
- Terrors and signs in the heavens
- Lawlessness
- Persecution
- Betrayal and martyrdom
- Hatred and lovelessness
- Nations surrounding Jerusalem for battle
- Preaching of the gospel to every ethnic group[15]

Today, we're seeing an increase of natural phenomena. Earthquakes, for example, are becoming more frequent and severe. 2023 saw the "highest death tolls for earthquakes since 2010" with "more than 64,100 deaths," and "over 59,000" of those occurring as a result of the 2023 Turkey–Syria earthquakes.[16]

Furthermore, we are witnessing an increase in violence and lawlessness that is devastating American cities. This, along with the COVID lockdowns and vaxxing policies, resulted in a mass migration of about two million people who fled America's largest cities from 2020 to 2022.[17] Of course, there's the influence of potential criminals among the mass of immigrants flooding our southern border. We're a nation of immigrants, and we embrace those coming to enjoy the freedoms we have in the US. However, we cannot overlook the very real possibility that some are not being properly vetted and could be criminals or desperate individuals who only add to the crime wave we seem to be experiencing. We've watched our digital screens and seen retail thieves ransacking major department stores, walking out in broad daylight with their take.

Additionally, our 24/7 news cycle is replete with pictures of war and its tragic effects. In 2022, Russia shocked the world with its invasion of Ukraine. In 2023, Hamas horrifically assaulted and murdered innocent Israeli civilians. And Israel then declared war on Hamas, which soon resulted in pro-Palestinian riots breaking out in the streets of many cities around the world. It also resulted in the great exposure of antisemitism in US colleges and universities. Some 73 percent of Jewish college students claim to have experienced antisemitism on their campuses.[18]

Antisemitism is the ancient hatred. It is diabolical. *The only thing stronger than the ancient hatred is the love of the Ancient of Days.* This is man's sin and man's hatred of one another reaching its apex. What started with Cain killing Abel has now escalated to 8 billion people on a planet at the same time, under the influence of the same spirit of the age. God destroyed the earth in the days of Noah because of such violence and lawlessness.

Jesus also said, however, that this gospel of the Kingdom is going to be preached to all the nations of the world. That word *nations* is the Greek word *ethnos,* and it means ethnic groups. It means every single ethnic group on the planet is going to hear the gospel. There is going to be a harvest unrivaled in world history that is going to take place in the last days because there is going to be a passionate Church whose heart is aflame with love for Jesus and whose people have foreheads like flint in the face of difficult times and amid a rebellious, debased, and unrighteous, Romans 1 culture that suppresses the truth.[19]

1. Acts 2:17.
2. Office of the Historian, Foreign Service Institute, "Creation of Israel, 1948," *Office of the Historian,* https://history.state.gov/milestones/1945-1952/creation-israel#:~:text=On%20May%2014%2C%201948%2C%20-David,nation%20on%20the%20same%20day./ (accessed January 12, 2024).
3. David Parsons, "The Miracle of Israel's Rebirth," *ICEJ,* https://www.icej.org/understand-israel/israel-updates/the-miracle-of-israels-rebirth/ (accessed January 13, 2024).
4. Isaiah 66:8.
5. Matthew 24:32.
6. See Jeremiah 8:12–14; 24:1–6; Hosea 9:10; Micah 4.
7. These numbers are based upon this book's year of publication—2024.
8. See Daniel 9–11.
9. Daniel 12:4.
10. See Exodus 31:3; 35:31.
11. Genesis 11:7–8.
12. People Groups, https://www.peoplegroups.org/ (accessed January 13, 2024).
13. Franklin Graham, "The World is Ripe for Harvest," *Billy Graham Evangelistic Association,* https://billygraham.org/story/the-world-is-ripe-for-harvest/ (accessed January 13, 2024).
14. "Missions Statistics: Have We Failed The Great Commission?" *Missionary

Portal, https://missionaryportal.webflow.io/stats/(accessed January 14, 2024).

15. See Matthew 24:4–7, 14; Mark 13:6–10; and Luke 21:10–12, 16.

16. Wikipedia contributors, "List of earthquakes in 2023," *Wikipedia,* https://en.wikipedia.org/w/index.php?title=List_of_earthquakes_in_2023&oldid=1192772342/ (accessed December 31, 2023).

17. Daniel De Visé, "Two million people fled America's big cities from 2020 to 2022," April 12, 2023, *The Hill,* https://thehill.com/homenews/3944865-two-million-people-fled-americas-big-cities-from-2020-to-2022/ (accessed December 31, 2023).

18. Ivana Saric, "73% of Jewish college students report antisemitism on campus the school year: ADL," Axis, November 29, 2023, https://www.axios.com/2023/11/29/antisemitism-college-campus-adl-survey-israel-hamas-war/ (accessed January 13, 2024).

19. See Ezekiel 3:9; Romans 1:18.

THREE
AS IN THE DAYS OF NOAH

JESUS GAVE another interesting insight for what we could expect at the end of the age. He said the end times would look similar to the days of Noah right before the flood. *What's going on in our culture around us, therefore, should be one of the most obvious and clearest indications that we may be living in the end times.* Jesus said:

> Concerning that day and hour no one knows, not even the angels of heaven, nor the Son, but the Father only. For *as were the days of Noah,* so will be the coming of the Son of Man. For *as in those days before the flood* they were eating and drinking, marrying and giving in marriage, until the day when Noah entered the ark, and they were unaware until the flood came and swept them all away, so will be the coming of the Son of Man.

> MATTHEW 24:36–39

A few things are going on in Jesus' comparison of the days of His return to the days of Noah. *First, just as no one knew when the flood in Noah's time was going to come, none of us will know the exact day of Jesus' return—that is, until the day we see Him here.*

People outside Noah's immediate family were oblivious to the fact that judgment would overtake them. Back then, they didn't even know what rain was because it hadn't rained on the face of the earth until the day it rained and the waters of the deep were released. Up until that point, a mist or kind of dew watered everything.

Second, we will be doing what we typically do when He returns. We will be eating, drinking, getting engaged, and marrying. And just as the flood caught the people of Noah's time by surprise, people are going to be caught off guard as they are busy about their everyday lives. In other words, life as we know it will simply be happening when Jesus arrives on the scene.

That's the immediate takeaway from what Jesus told His disciples through comparing the days of His return to the days of Noah. It's interesting to note that recent research conducted on Mount Ararat in Turkey by archaeologists may finally prove the "ship-shaped mound" which "bears a striking resemblance to a colossal ship" actually is Noah's Ark. If proven true, this could be a key sign pointing to the Lord's return because Jesus used Noah and the flood as a reference point for us. [1]

Let's look more closely at Noah's story and time to discover some important insights about the end times.

WICKEDNESS, VIOLENCE & CORRUPTION

Genesis 6:5 tells us that, in the days of Noah, man was wicked, and "every intention of the thoughts of his heart was only evil continually." Verses 11 and 12 provide further description: "the earth was corrupt in God's sight and filled with violence," and "all flesh had corrupted their way on the earth." The sickness of sin had become rampant. Sin, in fact, was pandemic. It was to the point that God "regretted that he had made man on the earth, and it grieved him to his heart."[2] Then the Lord said: "I will blot out man whom I have created from the face of the land, man and animals . . . , for I am sorry that I have made them."[3]

Though God saved a remnant of humanity and animals, the rest were drowned. That's what happened in Noah's day. "Everything on the dry land in whose nostrils was the breath of life died. . . . They were blotted out."[4] And when the Son of God returns, it will be that jarring as well. Zechariah 14:1–5 describes what happens when Jesus returns:

Behold, a day is coming for the Lord, when the spoil taken from you will be divided in your midst. For I will gather all the nations against Jerusalem to battle, and the city shall be taken and the houses plundered and the women raped. Half of the city shall go out into exile, but the rest of the people shall not be cut off from the city. Then the Lord will go out and fight against those nations as when he fights on the day of battle. On that day his feet shall stand on the Mount of Olives that lies before Jerusalem on the east, and the Mount of Olives shall be split in two from east to west by a very wide valley, so that one half of the Mount shall move northward, and the other half southward. And you shall flee to the valley of my mountains, for the valley of the mountains shall reach to Azal. And you shall flee as you fled from the earthquake in the days of Uzziah king of Judah. Then the Lord my God will come, and all the holy ones with him.

I do hope you just read that long portion of Scripture because, when the Lord returns, it will not be a picnic in June. The judgments of God are as beautiful as they are terrible and terrifying. Jesus' words in Matthew 24 about the floodwaters sweeping everyone away point to the judgments He will carry out in His return—judgments against kings and kingdoms, rulers and nations, and wicked and corrupt people.

Thank God, Jesus mentioned Noah by name. Why? Because his name speaks to us of God's mercy. His mercy found a righteous man—a man who "found favor" in His eyes.[5] That, of course, was Noah, whose name means resting place. *While everyone else was doing any and every wicked, chaotic thing they could imagine or think, Noah was countercurrent, counterculture. He was walking with God in righteousness.*

RADICAL OBEDIENCE

What does God do with a righteous man? God speaks to him. And God spoke to Noah, telling Noah of His plans and giving Noah specific instructions on how to build an ark.

Could you imagine living in a desert, having never seen rain, and being told to build a boat? There was no need for a boat. No oceans or seas nearby. He wasn't within a thousand miles of a body of water. And rain? What was rain?

But Noah was able to respond in obedience to the Lord. It was radical obedience, my friend. For the next 120 years, Noah labored on that boat. And it wasn't some little model-sized version. It was huge! It stood out as some circus oddity to the people around Noah. I'm sure they mocked and jeered him, and that for 120 years! When we look at 2 Peter 2:5, Peter called Noah "a herald of righteousness," so he must have been preaching and proclaiming to the people of the impending judgment. That's what a herald would do. For 120 years, "Noah did this; he did all that God commanded him."[6]

Even in the midst of a world of chaos, Noah built the ark. He partnered with God to save a remnant of people and animals. I think about the patience of God to give the world 120 years to repent from what He described as complete wickedness, corruption, and violence. The people didn't listen, but Noah did. Because he did, he and his family and many animals were "shut in" by God and were delivered from the flood.[7]

BE A RESTING PLACE

The days of Noah were a tipping point, an inflection point, that led to judgment. As the number of human beings were increasing in Noah's time, knowledge and wickedness were increasing proportionately—just like today. Some of the things that we are seeing in our world seem reminiscent to the days of Noah. What the Bible describes as good or righteous is now looked at as evil or extremism and fanaticism. If you're a Bible-believing Christian in this day, you're at odds with the general consensus about what is right, good, and ethical.

God found a resting place. His name was Noah. Noah believed that God would save in the midst of judgment. *Noah believed that, if he would invest his life, his energy, his resources—his blood, sweat, and tears—building something in radical obedience to God and in response to the judgment he knew was coming, he and his family would not get swept away.* And he became a resting place for the Lord even during days of judgment. He was a saving entity, a righteous man. And that's what God is looking for in us. He wants us to be resting places in the coming days of judgment.

Do You remember when Noah was in the ark and he was trying to determine whether the waters had receded? Noah released a dove as a means to know whether it was safe to get out of the ark. The dove brought back an olive branch, a symbol of peace, showing Noah it was safe to disembark.[8] The dove is also a symbol of the Holy Spirit. The Holy Spirit came and rested on the ark, on what Noah had built by faith. And I think sometimes we can have a tendency, when we think about the end times and we think about the last days, to be focused on getting out of here. We can develop an escapist mentality that says, "I'm ready, Lord. Come in with your Black Hawk or Chinook helicopter and get us out of here!" We want out before things get too difficult. *God is looking for a people who are loyal to Him, however. He wants a people who will go the distance, doing the work until He comes.* He longs for His people to believe Him, to partner with what He's doing. He is looking for those who are willing to build an ark, a resting place in their lives and in His Church. Why? Because He wants to find a place where He can send His glory—a place where His Presence is welcome and His Holy Spirit can come and rest.

During crisis, while all the judgments are being poured out and many are being swept away, the world will need some Noahs upon whom the Spirit of the Lord rests. It will need some faith-filled and faithful individuals who have built their lives anticipating the Lord's return and all that comes with it. Like Noah, they will be willing to be the odd person out. Listen, everybody thought Noah was crazy until the rain started falling. And the world might think you are crazy, but when judgments begin to come and things begin to shake and fall apart, those same people are going to be looking for a resting place and a safe place, and that's who God wants us to be. Don't get drowned in dissipation, but be a person found waiting in anticipation of Jesus' victorious return.

---

1. Walla! "New research might point out to the location, remains of Noah's Ark," The Jerusalem Post, November 1, 2023, https://www.jpost.com/archaeology/article-770948/ (accessed January 26, 2024). "The dimensions of the mound closely match the description of Noah's Ark in Genesis, '300 cubits long, 50 cubits wide, and 30 cubits high,' which translates to 157 meters in length, 26 meters in width, and 15 meter in height."
2. Genesis 6:6.
3. Genesis 6:7.
4. Genesis 7:22–23.
5. Genesis 6:8–9.
6. Genesis 6:22.
7. Genesis 7:16, 23.
8. See Genesis 8:11.

FOUR
ISRAEL: THE CONTROVERSY & THE TEST

Major controversies will be brewing at the end of the age. It is one of the most distinguishing hallmarks of the Lord's return. There will be a controversy with the nations, a controversy with Israel, and a controversy with God. The controversies will test the Church as a whole and individual believers as well. The question for us all will be this: *Will we stand with Israel as she is attacked on every side in an all-out assault from the nations and Satan?* The greatest persecution we face as believers at the end of the age will be in response to how we stand with and support Israel.

A COLLISION OF CONTROVERSIES

Before the return of the Lord, we know there will be wars and rumors of wars as Jesus told us. Nations and kingdoms will be fighting against each other, trying to exercise their sovereignty and keep their grip on power and land. They will also form allegiances to triangulate other nations. Psalm 2 depicts just what these kings and rulers will be doing:

> Why do the nations rage, and the people plot a vain thing? The kings of the earth set themselves, and the rulers take counsel together, against the Lord and against His Anointed, saying, "Let us break Their bonds in pieces and cast away Their cords from us." He who sits in the heavens shall laugh; the Lord shall hold them in derision. Then He shall speak to them in His wrath, and distress them in His deep displeasure: "Yet I have set My King on My holy hill of Zion."
>
> PSALM 2:1–6 NKJV

Zion's hill is the prime real estate the nations want, but it belongs to the coming King, the Son of God. Much of the spiritual battle at the end of the age is zeroed in on the nation of Israel, the Jewish people, and, in particular, the city of Jerusalem. The reason for that is because God has set His intentions and He has set His government to rule and reign from Mount Zion, which is Jerusalem. Psalm 2 gives us a prophetic picture of what happens as the end of the age grows closer and as the coming storm, as it were, begins to intensify.

Saint, you need to know the last days will be marked and even identified as a collision of these controversies among the nations, Satan, and God. Why do the rulers and the nations rage? According to Psalm 2, they're all conspiring together around one thing: They want to break off God's rule and His restraints. This doesn't rock God's world, though. In fact, we just read that His response to all this is laughter. God is laughing. He is laughing even now. Yet in the coming days, we're going to witness a massive collision, not just of cultures, but if we're looking at this through the lens of the Spirit, we're going to see a collision of controversies with the nations, with the rulers of those nations, and with Israel. Ultimately, God will deal with the nations and their respective rulers, He will deal with Israel, and He will deal in finality with Satan. He will resolve these controversies.

GOD'S CONTROVERSY WITH ISRAEL

God has a controversy with the people of Israel. We find a reference to this in Hosea 2:1–13. This controversy that God has with Israel is an ancient controversy. *It is a controversy based around Israel's continued unfaithfulness to her covenant promises to God.*

God had given the people of Israel the Promised Land. He had given them spiritual promises, and He had been faithful to keep covenant with them and keep His word to them. But Israel went after other gods. God summed up His controversy with these words, "'I will punish her for the days of the Baals to which she burned incense. She decked herself with her earrings and jewelry, and went after her lovers; but Me she forgot,' says the Lord."[1]

Thousands of years have passed, and God has faithfully sent prophets during those years to correct and redirect Israel. He even sent His Son to Israel, but over and over again, she has rejected God. He allowed her to go into exile, to be scattered among the nations. At the end of the age, however, He will resolve this controversy once and for all. He will regather "the outcasts of Israel" from the four winds of the earth, from every nation on earth.[2] He will do what He promised in Hosea 2:21–23: "And in that day I will answer, declares the Lord. . . . And I will have mercy on No Mercy, and I will say to Not My People, 'You are my people'; and he shall say, 'You are my God.'"

Already, as we have discussed as one of the game changers, this regathering has begun. The "First Aliyah" was "the first mass immigration wave to the Land of Israel after 2,000 years of exile," in which an estimated 30,000 Jews immigrated from Eastern Europe and Yemen "in the last quarter of the nineteenth century."[3] It was followed by the "Second Aliyah" at the beginning of the twentieth century, which brought an additional "35,000 Jews, mostly from Russia."[4] They began establishing Jewish institutions and forming settlements. Thousands of Jews immigrated to Israel in three more Aliyahs before 1948. That year, of course, Israel became a nation once again. Those who have been scattered are still returning to the land today.

The prophet Jeremiah told of the time when all exiles of Israel will return.[5] But then he said, "Alas! For that day is great, so that none is like it; and it is the time of Jacob's trouble, but he shall be saved out of it."[6] What is "the time of Jacob's trouble"? Jacob's trouble refers to the time when all the nations of the earth, led by the antichrist, will come and apply great pressure against Israel, seeking to destroy her. But, ultimately, Israel will turn her face toward God and will recognize and receive Jesus as her Messiah.[7]

THE NATIONS' CONTROVERSY WITH GOD

As I mentioned, the controversy the nations and their rulers have is with God and His sovereignty. They don't want to submit to Him as the King of kings and Lord of lords. They want to break free from Him. Basically, it is a replay of the Tower of Babel.

God is God, however. He can't help but be who He is. He is the same God today that He was when dealing with the people on the plain of Shinar. Any attempt to overthrow Him will be stopped. When the peoples gathered and built the tower, God scattered them because He would not allow them to usurp His sovereignty.

Like the people who built the tower, the kings and rulers of the nations want to gather. They want to exalt themselves against God. They want to be worshipped rather than worship God. They want their names to fill the earth rather than God's. They want to build their own city, their own tower, their own idol, their own religion, and their own kingdom. That same spirit that started at Babel is still very much at work. Paul called it "the mystery of lawlessness" that leads to delusion, that leads to rebellion, that leads to wrath.[8]

You need to know that this controversy that the nations have with God is expressed in hatred. It is diabolical in nature. It is satanic. It is expressed in the hatred of both Israel, the Jewish people, and ultimately the Church. It is imperative, then, for us as the Church to have a biblical lens when we look at what is taking place on the earth today and in the future. Though God loves the nations of the world, make no mistake about it, Israel is the "apple of His eye," which means the pupil and the focal point of His eye.[9] Why? It isn't because the Jewish people are better than anyone else or the nation of Israel is some ideal nation. It isn't. In fact, most of the people living in Israel live in unbelief. Not everything that they do is appropriate. Not everything is something we should sign off on, but *God has set His covenant faithfulness on that nation because of the covenant He made with Abraham* when He said:

Lift up your eyes and look from the place where you are, north-ward and southward and eastward and westward, for all the land that you see I will give to you and to your offspring forever. I will make your offspring as the dust of the earth, so that if one can count the dust of the earth, your offspring also can be counted. Arise, walk through the length and the breadth of the land, for I will give it to you.

GENESIS 13:14–17

God promised Abraham his seed would become an innumer-able nation, and God promised Abraham the land. Earlier in Genesis 12:3, God told Abraham, "I will bless those who bless you, and him who dishonors you I will curse, and in you all the families of the earth shall be blessed." God has kept that promise of blessing and cursing to this day. And He will deal once and for all with the nations and rulers that curse Israel and that cast off His restraints. When all the nations surround Jerusalem in that day of the final battle, the Lord "will seek to destroy all the nations that come against Jerusalem," and He "will go out and fight against those nations."[10]

SATAN'S CONTROVERSY WITH GOD

From the very beginning of creation, Satan has had a contro-versy with God. And throughout human history, Satan has sought to upend God's complete plan of salvation to redeem His creation. Satan views anyone connected in covenant rela-tionship with God as enemy number one. That means he has vehement hatred against the nation and people of Israel as well as the Church.

Antisemitism is very real. It is a manifestation of Satan's ancient hatred. Elie Wiesel, the Nobel Peace Prize winner, author, and Holocaust survivor, was asked to explain the continued existence of antisemitism. He said it is "an irrational disease. The unsolvable puzzle is that the world has changed in the last 2,000 years, and only anti-Semitism has remained. The only disease that has not found its cure is anti-Semitism."[11]

Why is this so? Because this is a spiritual battle that will rage until Satan is thrown into the abyss. And any leader, people group, or political entity that align with Satan's desire to cast off the restraints of God and thwart God's plan of redemption for the world will hate the Jewish people. We've seen it time and time again throughout history. The Marxists and the progressives have hated Israel and the Jewish people because Jews stand in the way of their desire to form a Utopian society without God. Stalinist Russia imposed the pogroms, in which Jews were rounded up and massacred. Then there was Hitler's Holocaust where millions were killed in the gas chambers of concentration camps. Then there's Hamas who carried out a massacre in October of 2023, and antisemitism suddenly came out in the open as thousands of pro-Palestinian protesters chanted in cities around the world, calling for the obliteration of Israel "from the river to the sea."

Remember, this is a spiritual battle where Satan has a controversy with God. We are not fighting people. We are not wrestling with flesh and blood. But the devil knows that by destroying the Jewish people, he and his legions are attempting to prevent the gospel from being preached in all the nations of the earth and to stop God from establishing His Kingdom from Jerusalem. That's what this is about. Satan has a controversy with God. He wants the earth.

In Revelation 12, we read about the dragon, that ancient serpent the devil, as he is in pursuit of the woman. The woman represents Israel, who gives birth to the male Child or the Messiah. "But the woman was given the two wings of the great eagle so that she might fly from the serpent into the wilderness, to the place where she is to be nourished for a time, and times, and half a time."[12] That's three-and-a-half years or 42 months. This is referring to the tribulation. But what I want you to see is what is in verse 15: "The serpent poured water like a river out of his mouth after the woman, to sweep her away with a flood." *This is an eschatological picture of the satanic hatred of the Jewish people that is allegorized as a river that flows out of the devil's mouth.* What typically flows out of our mouths? Words. What are the words pouring out of the serpent's mouth? Satanically inspired lies and antisemitic tropes. At the end of the age, the antisemitic words are going to be like a river, attempting to destroy and sweep Israel away.

In verse 17, the devil becomes "furious" with Israel and makes war on "her offspring, on those who keep the commandments of God and hold to the testimony of Jesus." So, this is a picture of the end of the age when the enemy rages against God's people—Jew and Christian—and the way Satan assaults is through hate speech, lies, and accusation. The enemy is going to pursue the Church, the woman's offspring, right along with pursuing Israel. The Church is the spiritual descendant that has received the promises, the patriarchs, the prophets, and even the Messiah from Israel. *The Church does not replace Israel, however.* This is critical to understand. It means we must have a biblical lens through which we view the Church's relationship with Israel and Israel's relationship with the Church. If we do not have that proper biblical lens, we're susceptible to deception.

THE REPLACEMENT LIE

Unfortunately, there is a large segment in the Body of Christ that has a posture and an attitude of antagonism toward Jewish people. This segment of the Church has accused Jewish people of having rejected and killed Jesus, and has espoused a lie that God has written off Israel. This segment of the Church has a theological conviction that the Church has superseded or replaced Israel so that the Church now assumes the role of God's covenant people. The theological conviction I'm talking about is known as supersessionism or replacement theology.

Beloved, replacement theology is a lie from the pit of hell. It has done more damage to the evangelism of Jews than any single issue, and we should not continue to tolerate it. It is a spirit of anti-Israel or anti-Jewish sentiment that crept into the Church over the last 2,000 years, and it led to much of the persecution of the Jews throughout the Middle Ages. Even during the Reformation, it was a dominant theology and has been taught in major seminaries since. Denominations today still hold to it.

The apostle Paul had something to say about how the Church should view Israel. When writing to the Roman believers, he asked them, "Has God rejected his people?"[13] And he answered his own question in the same verse—"By no means!" *Israel has not been cut off. She still has promises to inherit.* Paul said that Israel's stumbling resulted in the Gentiles being "grafted in."[14] And then he cautioned Gentiles not to get arrogant about being grafted in. He explained:

> Lest you be wise in your own sight, I do not want you to be
> unaware of this mystery, brothers: a partial hardening has come
> upon Israel, until the fullness of the Gentiles has come in. And in

this way all Israel will be saved, as it is written, "The Deliverer will come from Zion, he will banish ungodliness from Jacob"; "and this will be my covenant with them when I take away their sins."

ROMANS 11:25–27

For the most part, the Jews live in the land today in unbelief, and we know there is only one method of salvation—"And there is salvation in no one else, for there is no other name under heaven given among men by which we must be saved."[15] It's the name of Jesus. There is no other way to be saved. Paul was not saying that Israel has a distinct covenant whereby she is saved without going through Jesus. The "mystery" of Israel's salvation will come during a global event in which the eyes and the veil and the hardness of her heart will be pulled back. That event will occur at the end of the age. While Israel faces the rage of the antichrist and all the nations gathered around her to destroy her, Yeshua, her Messiah, will appear, and she will see Him. And she will believe Him and will be saved.

THE TEST

What will we do when all the venom and fire from the dragon's mouth starts heading, not only toward Israel and the Jewish people, but right directly at us? What happens when we come under the threat of persecution if we stand with Israel or with our Jewish friends? We must determine in our hearts now what we will do. When that crisis finally comes—when what we read about in Psalm 83 and Ezekiel 14 and 38 occurs—it will be too late to be prepared. We must be prepared now.

The "Jew hatred," as Elie Wiesel referred to *antisemitism*, and the antisemitic protests are only going to intensify until that day we see Jesus. So, there is no escaping the test we will face. We must choose with whom to stand. And, beloved, we must stand with Israel. We must intercede and fast for Israel. We need to be people of prayer. *We must not come off the walls of intercession until we see God make Jerusalem "a praise in the earth."*[16] We need to love the people of Israel. We still need to love the nations and pray for all people. Yet when we see people and nations rise up against the nation of Israel and the Jewish people everywhere, we must stand with Israel and the Jewish people. We must stand with the apple of God's eye.

During the storm of the tribulation, the Jewish people are going to have their eyes opened. And there is coming a great revival of the Jewish people to believe in Yeshua and be included back into the people of God. It will happen at the end of the age. We have a part to play in it by praying for it—to hasten the day of the Lord's return. If we will prepare the way by watching and praying, not only will we urge on the revival of the Jewish people at the end of the age, but we will accelerate the Lord's return.[17]

Dear saint, the Church, in our darkest hour and faced by protesters and haters that are pouring out their antisemitic filth like water over the globe, will be mature and full of the power of the Holy Spirit. Our eyes will be focused on our returning King, the Word will be implanted in our hearts, prayer-like oil will fill our lamps, and we will be standing in love to protect the Jewish people and the nation of Israel.

God has a controversy with Israel. He's going to settle it. The nations have a controversy with God. God's going to settle it. Satan has a controversy with God. And God's going to settle it, finally—once and for all!

---

1. Hosea 2:13 NKJV.
2. Psalm 147:2; Isaiah 56:8.
3. Aliyah is a Hebrew word meaning "ascent." It refers to immigration to Israel. "The First Aliyah," *The National Library of Israel,* https://www.nli.org.il/en/discover/israel/zionism/zionism-history/first-aliyah/ (accessed January 25, 2024).
4. "Second Aliyah," *Wikipedia,* https://en.wikipedia.org/wiki/Second_Aliyah/ (accessed January 25, 2024).
5. See Jeremiah 30:3.
6. Jeremiah 30:7 NKJV.
7. See Romans 11:26–27.
8. 2 Thessalonians 2:7–12.
9. Zechariah 2:8 (NKJV).
10. Zechariah 12:9; 14:3.
11. Rabbi Benjamin Blech, "Why do people hate Jews and Judaism?" *The Washington Post,* May 21, 2015, https://www.washingtonpost.com/national/religion/why-do-people-hate-jews-and-judaism-commentary/2015/05/21/52f934e8-ffd8-11e4-8c77-bf274685e1df_story.html/ (accessed January 19, 2024).
12. Revelation 12:14.
13. Romans 11:1.
14. Romans 11:17.
15. Acts 4:12.
16. Isaiah 62:7.
17. See Luke 3:4–6; 2 Peter 3:11-12.

FIVE
A MUST-HAVE MILITARY MINDSET

As we've learned in the last few chapters, the end times will not suffer cowards. No, they will require us to be prepared for battle. I cannot emphasize this enough. We are such lovers of comfort and peace at all costs that we've forgotten we were born into a spiritual war zone. And there is no demilitarized zone—no Switzerland—in this war. Having a military mindset, then, is a must! How we look at the world around us and how we live life in the war zone are critical to how we will make out in the end. Surviving and thriving during combat will require a game plan.

You know, we have a plan for everything, it seems. We have a plan for vacation. We have a five-year plan for business. We have a mission statement with visions and values for church. We even have a plan for how to run errands and make our way down the aisles of Costco. But do we have a war plan on how to stand against the enemy? On how to not only survive, but thrive in these last days?

Some of us would probably say, "Well, I'm just hoping for the best, and I'm trusting Jesus to take care of the rest." Of course, there's nothing wrong with trusting God to bring you through each and every battle. We need to trust Him for that, but *we can't afford to be casual in our daily lives when it comes to confronting and resisting our enemy.* Being casual will result in your becoming a casualty.

Well-meaning people who go to church and love Jesus get sniped off because they're not ready for battle. Sometimes, they get taken and become prisoners of war. Because they didn't have a military mindset, they had no battle plan. It is critical, then, to develop a military mindset, and that means you have to know your enemy, know your weaponry, exchange your current world-view, and think like a warrior.

KNOW YOUR ENEMY

In John 10:10, Jesus exposed three of the main activities of a thief. He said, "The thief comes only to steal and kill and destroy." These are the activities of the chief thief, the devil.

The devil is an equal opportunity destroyer. He doesn't play by the rules. He's not merciful. He plays in the shadows, camouflaging himself in everyday life. He'll even disguise "himself as an angel of light."[1] And as we'll discuss more thoroughly in chapter eight, he skillfully uses his number-one weapon of deception. Right now, he is plotting how, at the very least, to rob us of those things that are ours in Christ—things like peace, joy, love, patience, and self-control.[2] He's trying to steal our fruit!

Christian, whether you realize it or not, whether you want it or not, you are living in the enemy's crossfire. In fact, you're in the crosshairs of the devil's scope. I really feel it is my assignment to help you see who your enemy is and how you are one of the targets he wants to immobilize. You matter to the Kingdom of God, and the devil knows it. So, you ought to know he's not just some petty thief. He's a real killer!

But he's not flesh and blood. That's important for you to know as well. Furthermore, your fight is not against red-blooded humanity. The apostle Paul explained that our fight is "against the rulers, against the authorities, against the cosmic powers over this present darkness, against forces of evil in the heavenly places."[3] We're dealing with a created being, but not a human being. And we're dealing with those who are in league with him. These are the ones Paul said we're fighting against.

Ezekiel 28:12 described the devil as once being "the signet of perfection, full of wisdom and perfect in beauty." Verse 14 calls him "an anointed guardian cherub" that walked "in the midst of the stones of fire" on the mountain of God. But then he was expelled from heaven along with a third of the angelic hosts of heaven.[4] Why? Because of pride, corruption, wickedness, and violence.[5] He's got a motley crew all coming after you and me. But thanks be to God, we have some weapons to use against him.

KNOW YOUR WEAPONRY

After the apostle Paul told us about who and what we're fighting against, he said this:

> Therefore take up the whole armor of God, that you may be able to withstand in the evil day, and having done all, to stand firm. Stand therefore, having fastened on the belt of truth, and having put on the breastplate of righteousness, and, as shoes

for your feet, having put on the readiness given by the gospel of peace. In all circumstances take up the shield of faith, with which you can extinguish all the flaming darts of the evil one; and take the helmet of salvation, and the sword of the Spirit, which is the word of God, praying at all times in the Spirit, with all prayer and supplication. To that end, keep alert with all perseverance, making supplication for all the saints.

EPHESIANS 6:13–18

Whew! That's a lot of munition available to us. Let's take a minute to unpack our spiritual warfare locker and check out our military capabilities. If you'll notice, all the munition we've been given looks like it is defensive in nature. We have a belt, a breastplate, shoes, a shield, and a helmet. These are available to us for our protection.

There are two things we're given as offensive weapons. The first one mentioned is a sword, which is the Word of God. And what we know about that Sword is it is "living and active, sharper than any two-edged sword, piercing to the division of soul and of spirit, of joints and of marrow, and discerning the thoughts and intentions of the heart."[6] Now, that Sword works in the supernatural realm. It is some kind of smart weapon or precision guided munition (PGM). Paul wasn't talking about hitting someone with your Bible. He was talking about being in the Word, knowing the Word, and being able to use it defensively. That involves declaration and proclamation. It is powerful! It is a precise device.

There is another offensive weapon, and we'll be talking about that more throughout this book. It is prayer. In Ephesians 6, the apostle Paul spoke about praying in the Spirit, praying in tongues. That's very important to do in prayer because sometimes we don't know how to pray. Scripture tells us when we're in that kind of situation, the Holy Spirit helps us and "intercedes for us with groanings too deep for words."[7] So, Paul says to pray "at all times" and pray "with all prayer."

Soldier, know your weapons. Put on all of God's armor, wield the Word of God, and pray all kinds of prayer! That's going to help you stand and have a mindset to keep standing against your enemy, the devil.

EXCHANGE YOUR WORLDVIEW

Our worldview is very important to our lives in that it provides a framework for how we perceive the world we live in, or said another way, how we perceive reality. As Western thinkers, we have been greatly affected by the Enlightenment or the Age of Reason. Consequently, we tend to have a worldview that's largely based on logic and reason. That means we rely heavily on our five physical senses of smell, taste, touch, sight, and sound to navigate reality. If we can't physically sense something, then it isn't real. Or if we can't scientifically evaluate or prove something, then it isn't real, either. This results in our being very skeptical regarding the supernatural. Hollywood has influenced many Americans, however, so that they dabble with supernatural things like witchcraft or the occult. For the most part, though, we in the West come from a very materialistic and humanistic mindset that puts man at the center of the universe instead of God.

Interestingly, if we were to travel around the world and visit different nations, we would probably find 80 percent of these nations possess a supernatural worldview. Though they may understand natural laws, they also understand there is an unseen realm where personalities and powers and agendas affect the world in which we live. If you go to India, for example, Hindus have millions of gods. They believe in the supernatural. There are nations in Africa that are very animistic. They believe in nature, demons, spirits—theirs is a mixture—but they believe in the supernatural as well. Whether you go to nations in Asia or South America, you will find many who believe in the supernatural, too.

Friend, it is time for us to exchange our worldview. Not so that we can believe in or practice works of darkness or worship a multitude of gods, but so we can have God—the real God—at the center of our universe. So we can live aware, not fearful of, but aware of our adversary and what he is trying to do. So we can be combat ready.

What I'm talking about then is you and I having a biblical worldview. We need to see things through the lens of the Scriptures and under the tutelage of the Holy Spirit. We need to have what the apostle Paul prayed for the Ephesians—"that the God of our Lord Jesus Christ, the Father of glory, may give you the Spirit of wisdom and of revelation in the knowledge of him."[8] *We must know Jesus. We must have wisdom, revelation, and knowledge of Him given to us by the Holy Spirit. We need a biblical worldview.* And this comes from spending time with God and His Word.

Sometimes, I think we Christians live our lives as either practical atheists or utopians. The Christian "practical atheist" acts as though there is no spiritual or supernatural realm, which means they act as if there is no spiritual warfare or conflict. They live as if God is off in the distance somewhere, and the adversary is a figment of the imagination. The Christian "utopian" lives as if everything is going to be okay in the end.

There's nothing to worry about. "C'est la vie," they say. "Such is life. Whatever happens will happen. The will of God will be accomplished. It's all good. I'm simply out here living my best life now."

Can I just say both of these extremes are lies? God is near. He is not off in the distance. The adversary is real and not some figment of our imagination. Spiritual warfare is happening even as you're reading this line—even if you can't see it with your own eyes. And what's happening isn't all good! That's why it's time to exchange your worldview.

THINK LIKE A WARRIOR

We have to learn to think like a warrior. This requires us to have a steady diet of God's Word because that is how our minds are renewed and changed. We must "present [our] bodies as a living sacrifice" and "not be conformed to this world, but be transformed by the renewal" of our minds.[9]

Not only do we eat the Word to alter how we think, but we also "set" our minds on certain things or in certain ways. For example, the apostle Paul told the Romans that the ones "who live according to the flesh set their minds on the things of the flesh, but those who live according to the Spirit set their minds on the things of the Spirit."[10] He added, "To set the mind on the flesh is death, but to set the mind on the Spirit is life and peace."[11] *How we set our minds will either bring peace and life or anxiety and death. And how we set our minds is determined by our allegiance.* If our allegiance is to our flesh, we will serve our flesh; we will set our minds on our flesh. If, however, our allegiance is to God, then we will set our minds on Him, on His Spirit. And it also follows that we will submit ourselves to God, His Word, and His will.

In Philippians 2:5–8, we're encouraged to have the mind of Christ, who, though he was God, "did not count equality with God a thing to be grasped, but emptied himself, by taking the form of a servant. . . . And being found in human form, he humbled himself by becoming obedient to the point of death, even death on a cross." Jesus was humble and obedient. He did what He was instructed to do by His Father. That's the kind of mindset we should have. That's thinking like a warrior in the Kingdom of God.

We have to train our minds to think like our Master. And one great way to do this is by setting our "minds on things that are above, not on things that are on earth."[12] We also train our minds to think on certain things. In Philippians 4:8, the apostle Paul listed some things we can choose to think about like "whatever is true, whatever is honorable, whatever is just, whatever is pure, whatever is lovely, whatever is commendable," whatever is excellent, or whatever is "worthy of praise." I call this *basic training for the mind.*

If you want to be in the army of the Lord and be combat ready, you can't just go down to the recruiter's office and sign up. *You're not a warrior until you've gone through training.* You must understand authority. You must be able to await your orders and then do them. What we can do to train is know our enemy, know our weaponry, exchange our worldview, think like a warrior, and then act like one who is strong in the power of God's might and not our own.

---

1. 2 Corinthians 11:14.

2. See Galatians 5:22.
3. Ephesians 6:12.
4. See Luke 10:18; Revelation 12:4.
5. See Ezekiel 28:17–19.
6. Hebrews 4:12.
7. Romans 8:26.
8. Ephesians 1:17.
9. Romans 12:1–2.
10. Romans 8:5.
11. Romans 8:6.
12. Colossians 3:2.

SIX

THE BATTLE FOR THE ALTAR

THERE IS a story in the book of Judges about a man and his initial reservation to push back against his oppressors. His name was Gideon, and he was called of God to be a courageous leader in the battle for the altar of the Lord.

Gideon and the children of Israel were living in the aftermath of a cultural shift that changed how they viewed themselves and the nations around them. In fact, it totally changed their worldview as well because Israel had gone from being the people of God vanquishing the giants and kings occupying their Promised Land to a people hiding in caves with their tails between their legs. I mean, in the days of Joshua, Israel had miraculously taken possession of the land of her inheritance. Her people were dwelling in homes they had never built and eating from vineyards they had not planted. But then that generation left the scene while another one arose that "did not know the Lord or the work that he had done for Israel."[1] This new generation "did what was evil in the sight of the Lord."[2] To discipline them, God "gave them into the hand of Midian seven years."[3] And this is what the Midianites did to the children of Israel:

> Whenever the Israelites planted crops, the Midianites and the Amalekites and the people of the East would come up against them. They would encamp against them and devour the produce of the land, as far as Gaza, and leave no sustenance in Israel and no sheep or ox or donkey. For they would come up with their livestock and their tents; they would come like locusts in number—both they and their camels could not be counted—so that they laid waste the land as they came in. And Israel was brought very low because of Midian. And the people of Israel cried out for help to the Lord.
>
> JUDGES 6:3–6

The cultural shift that took place in Israel made them come under the influence of such an oppressive enemy that it made them go into hiding. These were farmers living in an agrarian culture. Their parents and grandparents before them were valiant and skillful warriors. But here they were planting each year with the expectation of a coming harvest only to have their harvest hijacked by the Midianites and Amalekites. And every year they were expecting the increase and multiplication of their livestock only to have them taken away by the same oppressors. *The Israelites had to be suffering from PTSD because they had endured such humiliation and subjugation for seven years.* It is one thing to have what they experienced happen just once. That's an anomaly. But when it happened year after year after year—all their hard work came to naught, and all their hopes and dreams were dashed—they went from angry to fearful to surrender. As a nation, they had gone from vanquishing to being vanquished. And they had given up. That's why they hid in caves.

CALLED OUT OF SURVIVAL MODE

It is in these bitter circumstances that we find Gideon. He's in the winepress with a bit of spare wheat, and he's trying to break off the stem without being seen. What does that tell us? It tells us that, just like the rest of Israel, he, too, had given up hope and switched into survival mode.

Unbeknown to Gideon, something was about to change. The Lord appeared to him, and the two had a telling conversation:

> And the angel of the Lord appeared to him and said to him, "The Lord is with you, O mighty man of valor." And Gideon said to him, "Please, my lord, if the Lord is with us, why then has all this happened to us? And where are all his wonderful deeds that our fathers recounted to us, saying, 'Did not the Lord bring us up from Egypt?' But now the Lord has forsaken us and given us into the hand of Midian." And the Lord turned to him and said, "Go in this might of yours and save Israel from the hand of Midian; do not I send you?" And he said to him, "Please, Lord, how can I save Israel? Behold, my clan is the weakest in Manasseh, and I am the least of my father's house." And the Lord said to him, "But I will be with you, and you shall strike the Midianites as one man."
>
> JUDGES 6:12–16

This was the prophetic calling of Gideon at one of the most crucial hours in Israel's history. And it isn't unlike the hour in which you and I are living. You see, I believe with all of my heart that the circumstances of Gideon and his calling are eerily emblematic of the twenty-first-century Church. And there was a bigger battle than a cultural or political battle. God wanted to raise up a prophetic voice who would turn the hearts of His people back to a devotion to Him. He also wanted them to see themselves as overcomers, rather than those who had been overcome. *The real battle that was going on, then, was not a battle for the wheat, and it was not a battle for the cave. Neither was it a battle for the cattle or the culture. It was the battle for the altar.*

What I think about when I look at the life of Gideon is *Gideon was found by God in the place of yesterday's new wine, searching for today's strength.* He was trying to break out of a survival mentality by going to the place where, at one time, there was an overabundance and flow of new wine. I think we in the Western Church have done something similar. As caretakers of revival and awakening stories or other moves of God, we've gone to the place of yesterday's new wine, hoping to find the strength and power that was once there. Tired of being looted and routed by our adversary, we've basically gone into survival mode, having not found today's wine. You can hear it in how we talk, "Well, I'm just trying to get through the day. I'm going to climb back up into my cliff, into my little stronghold, in my little cave with Jesus, put on a little worship, and make it one more day. Just going to stay in my cave because I'm tired of the enemy coming and stealing from me."

Beloved, the Church is suffering from PTSD. Yesterday's models do not work for today's challenges. All the tools and the implementation of our own strength in our own hand have failed us. And we've started to lose our hope. It is hard to even rise up in anticipation of the day we'll see our Lord face-to-face.

Listen, the thing that the devil steals the most is our hope and our expectation. If he can get those, he's going to take out our faith because "faith is the assurance of things hoped for, the conviction of things not seen."[4] The enemy loves to steal hope and to steal courage from the saints. *If he can steal courage from you and me, if he can steal courage from the people of God, he can imprison us as POWs in the Promised Land.* But God's answer every single time to circumstances like these is always courageous leadership. It is always calling leaders out of the winepress and into a greater place of courage.

CALLED TO COURAGEOUS LEADERSHIP

Gideon's name meant one who tears down or mighty warrior. So, when God showed up and called him by name, He was basically saying, "Gideon, remember what your name means." And I appreciate Gideon for his honest, straightforward questions he asked God, "Well, wait a second, Lord. If I'm a mighty man of valor, then I've got some questions for You. Number one, why has all this stuff happened to us? Why are we in the circumstances that we're in? Number two, where are all the miracles? I grew up in Sabbath school hearing about Moses and Joshua. Why have You allowed us to come under such oppression?" Gideon was courageous enough to ask God to His face, but notice that the Lord didn't answer Gideon's questions. The Lord didn't say, "Let Me explain to you why in My sovereignty and in My providence I've permitted this." Instead, the Lord just turned to Gideon and said, "Go in this might of yours."

But Gideon wasn't having it—"God, I'm not qualified. You're looking for a courageous leader. You've got the wrong address and the wrong guy. I'm the least in my father's house—the least in Manasseh, the weakest tribe in all of Israel."

The Lord didn't let Gideon win his argument. He called Gideon to live up to his name. "But I will be with you, and you shall strike the Midianites as one man."

If you've ever tried to lead anything, if you've ever tried to build anything or tried to raise a family even, it isn't like one gut punch knocks all of the strength out of you. It isn't like you woke up one day and decided to be a victim. *No, typically, we succumb to hopelessness when we've dealt with circumstance after circumstance or hardship after hardship—and that repeatedly over time.* Nobody just decides, "Today, I'm going to believe that I can't win." No, there's an inflection moment where you stop believing victory is possible, and that's when you lose hope. And the most valuable commodity that we have as leaders and children of God is hope. The Old Testament calls us "prisoners of hope."[5] Gideon, whose name spoke about the destiny God had for him, didn't believe it in his heart. He had lost hope. But God didn't give up on him.

A COURAGEOUS WARTIME LEADER

There are two kinds of leaders. There are peacetime leaders, and there are wartime leaders. Winston Churchill, to stick with our World War 2 theme from chapter one, was a wartime leader. If you've ever studied the life of Winston Churchill, the Prime Minister of the United Kingdom (UK) during World War 2, you'll know his earlier career as a soldier and a statesmen were underwhelming. It wasn't until Hitler came to power and the UK was thrown into a war in mainland Europe that Churchill's light began to shine and shine brightly.

Personally, I love Churchill's speeches, especially his first speech as prime minister in 1940. The speech was monumental and demonstrated what a wartime leader should look and sound like. Speaking to the House of Commons on May 13, 1940, Churchill "asked the House to declare its confidence in his Government. The motion passed unanimously."[6] He said:

I would say to the House, as I said to those who have joined this government: "I have nothing to offer but blood, toil, tears and sweat."

We have before us an ordeal of the most grievous kind. We have before us many, many long months of struggle and of suffering. You ask, what is our policy? I can say: It is to wage war, by sea, land and air, with all our might and with all the strength that God can give us; to wage war against a monstrous tyranny, never surpassed in the dark, lamentable catalogue of human crime. That is our policy. You ask, what is our aim? I can answer in one word: It is victory, victory at all costs, victory in spite of all terror, victory, however long and hard the road may be; for without victory, there is no survival. Let that be realised; no survival for the British Empire, no survival for all that the British Empire has stood for, no survival for the urge and impulse of the ages, that mankind will move forward towards its goal. But I take up my task with buoyancy and hope. I feel sure that our cause will not be suffered to fail among men.[7]

And it was speeches like this in the middle of one of the most hopeless moments in England that the mindset and the paradigm of the nation turned—all because of courageous wartime leadership. What's interesting is, as soon as the war was won, Winston Churchill's popularity went into decline. There was a period of time during crisis, during hopelessness, where all eyes were looking for someone to step forward and say, "Yes, it's dark. Yes, it's difficult. Yes, it's sobering, but we're going to fight until we win, and we will overcome." This is exactly what's needed today in the Kingdom of God. God is always raising up courageous prophetic leaders, whether it is a Gideon, an Elijah, or a John the Baptist. God will raise up those who are willing to say what no one else will say. He will bring to the forefront those who carry a groan of intercession and intervention, those who can see what nobody else can, those who can call the people of God to believe for something more.

Christian, the true measure of a leader is not the position he or she takes during times of peace. *The true measure of a leader is where he or she stands during moments of conflict and crisis.* Peacetime leaders look to diplomacy, negotiation, and compromise as a means of securing what they have, not knowing that by making that decision they've already lost the war. There is no virtue in detente. *Wartime leaders refuse to back down and understand that peace tomorrow in future generations will be the product of their courage and sacrifice today.* And that was what God was calling Gideon to be in his hour. God was calling Gideon to be a courageous wartime leader. God was calling him to be a leader with a mindset that—in spite of pain, in spite of fear, in spite of the challenges, in spite of the enemy—he would be brave and bold and valiant.

CALLED TO PULL DOWN THE ALTAR OF BAAL

We are living in a day when courage is discouraged and when consensus is *the* consensus. It takes a courageous wartime leader to stand out and step away from the fray, away from the winepress and say, "I'm not retreating to the caves. I'm pursuing the altar of the Lord because this is what God has told me to do." This is what Gideon finally agreed to do—to "pull down the altar of Baal" that his father had set up, "cut down the Asherah" that was beside it, and "build an altar to the Lord . . . on the top of the stronghold there."[8]

Why was God raising up a courageous wartime leader? Because the battle was over the altar. The battle that was being waged just wasn't some fight over economics or a battle against a physical enemy like the Amalekites and the Midianites. It was a battle for the altar of the Lord.

Today, like then, it is very easy for us to get our eyes on the Midianites or the Amalekites, on the economy, on the elections, or on our micro challenges. When we do, we miss the bigger battle. In our culture and in the Church in America, I believe the battle is for the altar of the Lord. Whose altar will be allowed to stand? The altar of Baal or the altar of the Lord? And why would God raise up a prophetic people in this hour? I believe it is to tear down the altar of Baal, and it is to rebuild and reestablish the altar of the Lord. It is time for the Church to shift from survival mode and hear God's call.

For us to get there, we have to understand that there are two spirits at work in this generation. First John 4:6 speaks of the two: the spirit of error versus the Spirit of truth. I call the spirit of error *the spirit of this age*. It is a deceptive spirit versus the Holy Spirit. And here is what's dynamic about this. These two are also at work within the Church.

During Gideon's life, Israel as God's covenant people had synchronized their devotion to Yahweh with devotion to Baal. The two weren't even separate. The people had tried to combine them together.

And what they didn't realize, for example, was that the Asherah pole beyond the altar was actually a deity. It was a representation of the spirit that was the dominant influence in the culture. So, what was going on over the course of time was the influence of the surrounding nations and their idols and their gods began to influence Israel. The alternative, dominant, counterfeit spirit was the spirit of Baal. And it was the altar to Baal, the altar Gideon's father had built, that God commanded to be torn down.

Throughout the Old Testament, Baal had many different names, but it was the same spirit. And it is the same spirit manifesting in a lot of things in our culture today. It is in education, in social media, in business, and in our homes. We watch what comes out of Hollywood, and we see what's going on in schools and in the news cycle. Those are just physical manifestations of a spiritual influence that I believe is the exact same spirit that Gideon was confronting in his day. It is the same spirit that God's people are always having to confront because I'll tell you that *the spirit of Baal is actually the alternative counterfeit to the spirit of revival that the Holy Spirit—the Spirit of truth—brings.*

Here are some details about Baal that are of note. His name as a verb means to marry, and his name as a noun means the one who has dominion over the dominant one. He's the owner master. Typically, in the Old Testament, he was the god of the storm and of rain. Why was that important? When you are a farmer and you make your money based on the success of your crops and your cattle, the god of the storm is an appealing god to worship because you need rain for your crops and feed for your herds. Your crops and your herds are tomorrow's prosperity. Baal was called the god of the rain, which touched three primary issues: climate, economy, and sexuality. He was the bringer of rain, the bringer of success and fertility.

Why is that a counterfeit to the spirit of revival? Because Zechariah 10:1 says, "Ask rain from the Lord in the season of the spring rain, from the Lord who makes the storm clouds." And in Acts 3:19–20, we read, "Repent therefore, and turn back, that your sins may be blotted out, that times of refreshing may come from the presence of the Lord." Then Hosea prophesied, "Sow for yourselves righteousness; reap steadfast love; break up your fallow ground, for it is time to seek the Lord, that he may come and rain righteousness upon you."[9]

In Scripture, revival is always typified as rain. Baal, the god of rain, therefore, is the counterfeit to revival. So, think about the modern equivalent of Baal. What dominant message in our time focuses around climate, economy, and sexuality? Our culture is calling for people to control and affect the climate in order for us to have a thriving economy. And our culture is all about expressing sexuality. What is that? What's behind that? It is the spirit of Baal.

In the Old Testament, the way they served Baal, to get Baal to answer them, was to cut or emasculate men, to perform perverse sex acts, and to offer up children in sacrifice. The real problem is, just like Israel, the Church has synchronized the spirit of Baal with the spirit of revival. We say, "We'll worship God on Sundays, but we're putting our energy and our ideology and our thoughts and our politics and our childrearing and our sexuality and our finances and even our views on gender and life on the altar of Baal." What has that produced? We have entire denominations that used to be rooted in revival movements from the times God raised up courageous prophetic leaders like John Calvin, John Knox, and John Wesley, but yet now the altars upon which revival fires burned have been replaced by altars of Baal. And now we're seeing denominations rooted in revival movements walk away from the Faith. Some assert they see the Bible as an archaic book that doesn't really mean what it says. And they've made accommodations so as to have a place at the table of culture and be recognized as being culturally relevant and inclusive. You know what that is? That's Baal, the one who dominates, whose service required Israel to submit to it and go on living in their caves. It is the spirit of Baal, Israel allowed it, and we in our American culture and in the Church have allowed it.

But God called Gideon to be a courageous wartime leader. He ordered him to tear down the altar of Baal. And *God is searching for a generation of leaders who will bring reformation to the Church so that He can bring transformation to her and to our culture.* And here's the mandate that God gave Gideon. It is the mandate that He gives to all courageous leaders. I believe it is the mandate for you and me. Make no mistake about it, it is going to take courage, pastor. It is going to take courage, worship leader. It is going to take courage, Mom and Dad. It is going to take courage, missionary. You're going to have to be courageous, high school or college student. *The mandate for courageous leaders is twofold: Deconstruct the altar of Baal and rebuild the altar of the Lord.*

---

1. Judges 2:10.
2. Judges 6:1.
3. Ibid.
4. Hebrews 11:1.
5. Zechariah 9:12.
6. Wikipedia contributors, "Blood toil, tears and sweat," *Wikipedia,* https://en.

wikipedia.org/w/index.php?title=Blood,_toil,_tears_and_sweat&ol-did=1180400322/ (accessed January 17, 2024).

7. Winston Church, "Blood, Toil, Tears and Sweat," *House of Commons*, May 13, 1940, *International Churchill Society*, https://winstonchurchill.org/resources/speeches/1940-the-finest-hour/blood-toil-tears-sweat/ (accessed January 15, 2024).

8. Judges 6:25–26.

9. Hosea 10:12.

SEVEN

REVIVAL: REBUILDING THE ALTAR OF THE LORD

GOD WILL NOT SHARE His glory with some false god or idol, especially among His people or within His Church.[1] Though He may be patient and slow to anger, allowing time for His sons and daughters to come to their spiritual senses and repent, He will deal with us, coming to us "like a refiner's fire and like fullers' soap," and He will do so suddenly.[2] *As the Lord did with Gideon, the Lord will draft and deploy a courageous wartime leader upon whom He will put His glory and His Spirit.* That leader will contend against the spirit of Baal, tearing down the counterfeit altar, and will set the stones in proper order on the altar of the Lord in the house of the Lord.

You see, we've tried to build the altar our way, and God has rejected it because it isn't His altar. It's ours. If we build His altar according to His instructions, He will come. He will not come to people who are indifferent toward Him. He will not come where He is merely tolerated. The Lord shows up where

He is wanted, where He is welcome, where He is revered as God, and where He is celebrated.

I believe we're going to see God pour out His Holy Spirit, and it won't be so that we can build a subculture of revival in the Church. No, this outpouring will awaken the Church. *His outpouring will lead to a global awakening and a harvest of tens of millions of souls in one generation.* And it is going to change the landscape in a marked way. I believe that's what's coming.

If we will give our lives to tear down the altar of Baal and build the altar of God, we will set the stage for greater glory than we've ever experienced before. This is in the heart of God. We're not trying to convince God to do something He doesn't already want to do. God has been trying to get our generation's attention. He spent the last four or five years asking, "Have I got your attention yet? Oh, you thought you lived in one of those nations in which this could never happen? Have I got your attention now? Will you do it My way? Now, will you turn to Me with all of your heart?"

The mandate for courageous leadership, the Gideon mandate, begins with deconstructing the altar of Baal. To do so, we must:

1. Contend for the Faith.
2. Expose the works of darkness.
3. Destroy the strongholds of the enemy.

CONTEND FOR THE FAITH

We hear a lot about deconstruction these days, especially as it is applied to a person's beliefs or faith. The deconstruction I'm talking about is tearing down the altar of Baal, exposing the spirit that is at work, and showing the weakness and the fallacy of it. And that begins with courageous leaders who are willing to contend for the Faith, once and for all, delivered unto the saints. We must teach the Word and teach it unashamedly. We can't teach the Word through inspiring, self-help, positive-only teaching of the Bible. We can't take an X-Acto knife to the Word and say, "Oh, people love this verse, 'I can do all things through Christ who strengthens me.'" And then we don't state the fact that Paul wrote those words while imprisoned.

We must defend the Faith. To do so, we must stop letting TikTok theologians train our young people and teach them what the Bible says about every issue because we're afraid to touch on uncomfortable or off-putting issues. *The very reason why a generation is messed up and confused is because we've allowed the spirit of the Amalekites and the Midianites to come in and steal our children's inheritance. Because we didn't stand up courageously to disciple our own children, other voices jumped at the chance and did.* Make no mistake about it, our kids are being discipled. It's just a question by whom.

Furthermore, we've spent thirty years trying to build environments to make people who are lost comfortable. We're reading the "nice" verses out of the Bible. It's like chicken soup for the soul or fortune cookie theology. "You're going to have an amazing future. God's got a wonderful plan for your life." Oh, have you read Matthew 16:24? "Take up your cross and follow Me. Deny yourself. It's going to cost you something. It's going to hurt."

We've handicapped a generation because we've not shared the true and straightforward gospel. We've probably given people only a third of the Word, if that.

The Bible is redemptive from beginning to end, but we've got to be willing to deconstruct the altar of Baal stone by stone. Let me tell you why. *The lie of the enemy that is pervading our culture right now will destroy your life.* It's a subtle lie from the spirit of Baal. The Church has fallen prey to believing it, and the lie is this: The Holy Spirit can transform anybody's life unless they're gay, unless they're trans, unless they're using different pronouns to identify themselves. If you're an addict, Jesus can set you free. If you're a liar, Jesus can change you. If you're an alcoholic, Jesus can transform your life. If you're sexually promiscuous, He can set you free and give you new purity. But if you struggle with same-sex attraction, or if you're struggling with your identity, the Church's message seems to be, "Hope for the best." Or worse yet, "You can love Jesus just the way you are and stay as you are." This is a toxic lie from the spirit of Baal—from the pit of hell.

Yes, Jesus does love the people He created. And He "shows his love for us in that while we were still sinners, Christ died for us."[3] But He died to deliver us from bondage—all bondage. He died to deliver captives and set them free from Baal's lies. "He is able to save to the uttermost those who draw near to God through him, since he always lives to make intercession for them."[4] Jesus stands and says, "Every drop of My blood on the cross is more powerful than the biggest lie of the enemy. I can deliver you from any, every, and all bondage." That's how much He loves the world.

How have we believed the subtle lie? How can we be silent on these issues? It is because we don't know the truth of God's Word. If we knew it, believed it, and obeyed it, then we would know we are not called to condemn people in their sin, but we are called to set them free. We're called to walk with people, to disciple people, to offer the grace of God to people, but we've hidden in the stronghold, in the caves of this culture.

You know what that is? *Without even knowing it, the Church has come under the influence of the spirit of Baal, and entire denominations now are willing to actually change their theology rather than grow in their power.* Thankfully, Jesus is still working redemptively in His Church. He is still building His Church, "and the gates of hell shall not prevail against it."[5]

We must contend for the Faith. We must know the Word, believe the Word, preach the Word, teach the Word, and share the Word with the lost. It is their only hope. We must stand for truth at all costs, and we must not shy away from controversy when it comes to right and wrong—heaven and hell. We must love our neighbors, our families, our churches, our cities, and our nations, not withholding the love and goodness of God from them.

EXPOSE & DESTROY

The other two actions we must take go in tandem. We need to expose the works of darkness and then destroy the strongholds of the enemy. Of course, we're not looking to be unkind and expose people and their sin. However, we must bring the works of darkness into the light of God. And once the works are exposed, we cannot leave them exposed. No, we have to move into enemy strongholds and take them out.

Where are strongholds most often built by the enemy? It is in the mind. *The father of lies ensnares us with a lie—one that we believe—and then we build belief systems and structures in our thinking that become strongholds for the enemy.* We can't see these erector sets of our minds, but they are there. In addressing such strongholds, the apostle Paul wrote:

For though we walk in the flesh, we are not waging war according to the flesh. For the weapons of our warfare are not of the flesh but have divine power to destroy strongholds. We destroy arguments and every loft opinion raised against the knowledge of God, and take every thought captive to obey Christ, being ready to punish every disobedience, when your obedience is complete.

2 CORINTHIANS 10:3–6

This is real deconstruction. It is a war against arguments, lofty opinions against the knowledge of God, and disobedience to God's Truth. We have to take captive every thought that's running amiss and bring it under obedience to Christ.

I want you to notice something here if you haven't already. *An altar is an elevated structure on which worship is offered.* It is a sacred place. Though Gideon's family altar to Baal was an external, physical altar, the words of Paul tell us how altars can be within us. They're constructs of our minds and imaginations that our hearts yield obeisance to. The works of darkness come from minds that have believed a lie. That belief in a lie works itself out in more thoughts and then deeds of darkness. We need to be people of the light. We need to be people of the Word of God. We need our minds to be renewed. We need to deconstruct the altars within our hearts and minds, exposing them to the Word and light of God.

FULFILLING THE GIDEON MANDATE

To fulfill God's mandate to him, Gideon not only had to deconstruct the altar of Baal, but he also had to build the altar of the

Lord. Legalism and fundamentalism will always sign on to deconstruct the altar of Baal, but as soon as you begin to talk about building the altar of the Lord, all the fundies get really uncomfortable because *the altar of the Lord is the place where the supernatural Presence of God meets the people of God. It is the place where heaven and earth intersect.* It is the place where we pray, where we worship, and God makes Himself known.

In Judges 6:26, Gideon was given instructions to build on top of the stronghold "with stones laid in due order." These instructions point to God's desire to properly establish His altar right on top of the former stronghold that had been destroyed. *For us today, I propose this part of fulfilling the Gideon mandate means putting the Presence of God back at the center of Jesus' Church.* This means the practice of thanksgiving, adoration, exaltation, inter- cession, and prayer come back front and center. What the Lord was trying to say to Gideon was the way an army gets prepared to go and defeat the enemy out in culture is to construct the altar of the Lord inside the community of the people of God. It isn't enough for you to know what you're against. You have to reprioritize what you're for.

Jesus is wanting to get a distracted Church to put her eyes fully back on Him, to welcome Him. He wants to be enthroned on the praises of Zion and to awaken the Church to be a praying Church, to see the altar of the Lord, the place of prayer, as the place where courage fills our hearts. He wants us to restore the primacy of God's Presence, not only in our individual hearts, but in our corporate gatherings.

God wants us to remove the impurities of syncretism and accommoda- tion, and to rebuild the altar of corporate prayer so that we can release an army of courageous saints. He wants churches that pray, churches that prioritize His Presence, churches that prioritize worship that's pleasing to Him. God wants us to give Him room when we come together and for us to listen to what He wants to say to us. You see, syncretism shows up because we take worship and make it about us. If we will put Jesus back on full display and worship, true worship, and if we will call our church to pray, God's Presence will once again be honored and prioritized for His glory and honor.

God is building a people who will have courage to pray and seek Him. He promised long ago that, if His people who are called by His name will humble themselves, pray, seek His face, and turn from their wicked ways, He would then hear from heaven, forgive their sin, and heal their land.[6] Beloved, it is time to pray and turn and seek. If we have the courage in our hearts to believe His promise and then act on it, He will heal our land, He will forgive our sins, and He will revive His Church.

REVIVAL & NATIONAL AWAKENING

After Gideon rebuilt the altar of the Lord, Israel went into attack mode against the Midianites with an army of 300 men who lapped water with their hands.[7] God had whittled down this group of men from 10,000 because He had said the 10,000 were too many.[8]

With this army of only 300, God's plan was for them to attack at night, each man bearing a torch inside a jar in one hand and a trumpet in the other. Upon command, they broke their jars, causing their torches to shine, and blew their trumpets at once. Between the sound of all the jars breaking, the bright lights, and the blasts of the trumpets, the Midianites were confused, started fighting against each other, and fled.[9] That's how God, Gideon, and 300 men defeated the Midianites. My favorite part of the story is what the men did after they blew their trumpets. Courage suddenly swelled among the ranks of these former "cavemen" as they declared, "A sword for the Lord and for Gideon!"[10]

You know what God had done? God had infused their hearts with courage. He had pulled together a remnant of people who had once hid in caves, scared of their enemy. Once the altar of the Lord was rebuilt and in proper order, the cowardice turned to courage, and they were unified and ready for battle. Instead of dwelling in a defensive mode, they went on offense and defeated the enemy.

In Judges 7, Israel's culture was transformed as a result of the rebuilding of God's altar and the ensuing victory against her enemy. While Judges 6 brought revival, Judges 7 brought national awakening. That couldn't have happened if it weren't for one man who stood out of the winepress and said, "I believe You, God. If You'll go with me, if Your Presence will be with me like You promised, I'll go wherever You want me to go."

This is what God is calling His Church to do. We are at our winepress moment with the Lord. He is ready to equip His leaders and His army. He wants to infuse us with hope, faith, vision, courage, and conviction so that His glory can be seen upon us. I can see Him standing over the winepress of the American Church and looking down at the leadership. He is calling my name, He is calling your name, and He is saying, "You mighty man of valor," or "You mighty woman of valor, I want you to pull down the altar of Baal and rebuild My altar."

God's Presence is the X factor. His Presence and His courage are personified in the Person of the Holy Spirit. For Gideon, that courage from the Spirit of God was a product of intimacy. That's why, when Gideon was trying to figure out how and why God would choose him, and how God would dare call him to be a culture shifter and an altar builder, God's answer was that He would be with Gideon. Courage came out of that.

I don't know about you, but something about the story of Gideon makes faith and confidence arise in my heart that convinces me the global Church is on the precipice of an awakening like we've never seen. I believe it way down deep in my bones. How can I say that? Well, I've got evidence, and it is this. Throughout history, God has shown up in the darkest moments. Right when the enemy was making his moves under the cover of darkness, God was already working His counteroffensive. I've read the stories in Scripture of His revivals. I've read plenty of books on the subject until I'm ruined for anything less than a full deluge of the rains from heaven.

I've seen where God loves to take places like Wales, in the darkest hour in Europe, in the most apathetic, complacent place on the planet, and set a guy named Evan Roberts (1878–1951) ablaze for His glory. Roberts cried out to God to use him for His purposes. That sparked a revival that shut down sports for two years.[11] Conviction was hitting people as they went about their daily lives. People were getting saved. The Welsh revival saw 100,000 people converted.[12]

Then, I've read about Charles Finney (1792–1875) and intercessor Daniel Nash (1775–1831) and how God used them in the Second Great Awakening. Finney is often credited with around 500,000 converts.[13] I've read about John Wesley (1703–1791) and his good friend George Whitfield (1714–1770) and how God used them in the First Great Awakening. It resulted in 20,000–50,000 converts in New England.[14]

I could continue to name those whom God has used to spark fires of revival but would not be able to do justice to their stories. Volumes have been written for our edification and encouragement. Please go read them as they remind us of God's willingness to visit one person, thousands of people, an entire nation, and even a generation.

God is not looking for perfect conditions. He is looking for obedient people. I think of the more recent outpouring in February of 2023 at Asbury University in Wilmore, Kentucky.[15] A little town of about 1,500 people suddenly was inundated with 10,000-plus people on some nights, filling every sanctuary on campus. People lined up in the grass waiting to get in one of the sanctuaries. Traffic signs reading, "Closed for revival," were posted. No big-named preachers, no big-named worship leaders, no celebrities whatsoever were leading the meeting. It was led by Gen Z students who just showed up to pray and sing simple songs. No fanfare but the Presence of God coming day after day and night after night. People were confessing and repenting and receiving grace and forgiveness.

I think what took place at Asbury is a light spray of rain on the windshield of an American generation that has been in the winepress too long. And God says, "I'm able to do exceedingly abundantly above all that you could ever ask or think.[16] I'm just looking for a people like Gideon who will come up out of the winepress and say, 'If You are with me, God, I will do whatever You ask me to do. I'm not going to allow my identity to be defined by my experience and my defeat in the past. Lord, if You're with me, then I believe You. If Your Presence will go with me, then I'll go wherever You want me to go.'"

I believe God is looking for a generation in the Church that is defined by Him and not culture. The God who created us is the God who called us and is the only One who is allowed to define us and empower us. And that's why God is bringing us to the threshing floor. He is allowing us to be sifted. The sifting is bringing things to the surface. Church leaders are being confronted, and sin is being revealed. The old paradigms won't work in this new hour because God is doing something new and fresh. He is allowing the pressure to be applied to us. And that's revealing all our valleys and mountaintops and crooked places. God is doing this to bring correction—so that His mercy and grace can restore us.

Beloved, this is the only way for us to become ready for what He is about to do on a global scale. He wants to prepare us for the greatest harvest of souls. So, He must bring awakening and reformation to His people. Conviction, hunger, healings, miracles, signs, wonders, deliverances, and salvations will all be part of the great revival in the last days. What we have seen in awakenings and revivals past will go both local and global. It is coming, my friend, and we must be ready for it. It is going to come even as the adversary is releasing his nuclear warhead of deception.

---

1. See Isaiah 42:8.
2. Malachi 3:2.
3. Romans 5:8.
4. Hebrews 7:25.
5. Matthew 16:18.
6. See 2 Chronicles 7:14.
7. See Judges 7:6.
8. See Judges 7:3–4.
9. See Judges 7:19–21.
10. Judges 7:20.
11. "The 1904 Welsh revival," *The Bible College of Wales,* https://www.bcwales.org/1904-welsh-revival/ (accessed January 20, 2024).
12. Wikipedia contributors, "1904–1905 Welsh revival," *Wikipedia,* https://en.wikipedia.org/wiki/1904%E2%80%931905_Welsh_revival/(accessed January 19, 2024).
13. "Charles Grandison Finney: Did you Know?" *Christianity Today,* https://www.christianitytoday.com/history/issues/issue-20/charles-grandison-

finney-did-you-know.html/ (accessed January 18, 2024). According to this article, Finney is "directly, or indirectly credited" with 500,000 converts.

14. Wikipedia contributors, "First Great Awakening, *Wikipedia,* https://en.wiki pedia.org/wiki/First_Great_Awakening/ (accessed January 19, 2024).

15. "What Happened at Asbury University?" *Asbury University,* https://www. asbury.edu/outpouring/ (accessed January 20, 2024).

16. See Ephesians 3:20 NKJV.

EIGHT

DECEPTION: HELL'S NUCLEAR WEAPON

THE ENEMY DOESN'T HAVE new tricks because the old ones work. Our enemy, the devil, is crafty. He is scheming. He is wily. And from Genesis to Revelation, we read about his trickery and deceit—this "deceiver of the whole world."[1] It is no wonder, then, that *the enemy's primary tactic and most powerful weapon is deception.* Satan roams about the earth looking for those whom he can deceive and thereby devour. And in the last days, the spirit of deception and delusion will run rampant.

We've reviewed what Jesus told His disciples in Matthew 24, but it bears repeating, "Many will fall away and betray one another and hate one another. And many false prophets will arise and lead many astray. And because lawlessness will be increased, the love of many will grow cold."[2] And we've discussed 1 Timothy 4:1–2 about those who will leave the Faith, "devoting themselves to deceitful spirits and teachings of demons." But there is another portion of Scripture I want to draw your attention to that deals with the heart condition of people in the last days. Let's look at 2 Timothy 3:1–5.

> But understand this, that in the last days there will come times of difficulty. For people will be lovers of self, lovers of money, proud, arrogant, abusive, disobedient to their parents, ungrateful, unholy, heartless, unappeasable, slanderous, without self-control, brutal, not loving good, treacherous, reckless, swollen with conceit, lovers of pleasure rather than lovers of God, having the appearance of godliness, but denying its power. Avoid such people.

Now, that's some list! But if we take a closer look at Paul's list, we see that the real issue is going to be a love issue. *There will be a tipping scale, where people's hearts move from loving God to loving themselves and everything that goes along with that.* Why? Because at the end of the age, something is going to affect our hearts and tip the scales, if we're not careful, that is. What's going to do that? It is lawlessness. It is what Gideon faced when the enemy kept coming and stealing from him and his people. And *lawlessness is basically a lack of respect for authority.* It is a result of a diabolical lie that says, "Authority is not good. Authority will keep me from getting what I want." Lawlessness will lead to heartlessness, where a person has no care or love for anyone.

CORRUPTED LOVE

The warhead of deception goes straight to the heart. It gets into our hearts without our knowing it because it is stealth. Before it detonates completely, however, it corrupts our hearts. It is like a dirty bomb with radioactive material that changes our affections. The Bible talks about our hearts as the seat of our affections, where everything tilts toward ourselves and our pleasure. What is the radioactive material that changes our affections? It is corrupted love.

The apostle John was writing to Christians in the first century. He told them in 1 John 2:15, "Do not love the world or the things in the world. If anyone loves the world, the love of the Father is not in him." Although we know John 3:16 tells us God loves the world, the apostle John was not talking as Jesus was about the people in the world. In 1 John 2, John was telling the early Christians not to love the world's system. In verse 16, he clarified what is in the world, "the desires of the flesh and the desires of the eyes and pride of life." And verse 17 tells us, "The world is passing away along with its desires." In other words, everything in this world—that is "of this world"—that we're tempted to love is passing away. We can't be in love with the world and keep our hearts fervent in love for God.

That dirty bomb of deception with its radioactive corrupted love is meant to misdirect our affections—to cause us to love the world and the stuff in it. The devil looks for areas of vulnerability in our affections. He places worldly things in front of us that could draw our attention away. As James wrote, "Each person is tempted when he is lured and enticed by his own desire. Then desire when it has conceived gives birth to sin, and sin when it is fully grown brings forth death."[3] So, the devil loves to show us the desires of our eyes and flesh, and he likes to stroke the pride of our lives. That's how the corrupted love does its dirty work and how deception is detonated.

If that's true, then how do we keep our hearts from deception? How do we keep ourselves from our love becoming corrupted?

KEEPING YOUR HEART FROM DECEPTION

The book of Jude has some great insight for us on how to keep our hearts from deception and the dirty bomb of corrupted love.

> But you must remember, beloved, the predictions of the apostles of our Lord Jesus Christ. They said to you, "In the last time there will be scoffers, following their own ungodly passions." It is these who cause divisions, worldly people, devoid of the Spirit. But you, beloved, building yourselves up in your most holy faith and praying in the Holy Spirit, keep yourselves in the love of God, waiting for the mercy of our Lord Jesus Christ that leads to eternal life.
>
> JUDE 1:17–21

Jude's words tell us to remember what the apostles taught. There will be people in the last days whose love is corrupted, and their lives are misdirected as a result. They're people who do not have the Spirit of the Lord. But then Jude's words remind us we have the Spirit of the Lord. And according to Jude's admonition, there are three things we can do to keep from becoming those whose love has become corrupted. This is what we can do to keep our hearts from deception:

1. Build ourselves up in our faith.
2. Pray in the Holy Spirit.
3. Keep ourselves in the love of God.

There are a number of things we can do to build ourselves up in our faith. We can practice the Presence of God. I'm talking about having a real devotional life, where you daily sit in His Presence, pray, and worship Him—where you wait to hear what He has to say to you. Hearing the Word is a faith builder, and you can do that by reading it aloud. Romans 10:17 says, "Faith comes from hearing, and hearing through the word of Christ." And that points to another thing you can do to build faith, and that's becoming a part of a vibrant church family, where you can go and hear the Word as well as fellowship and worship with other believers. That's an excellent way to build your faith. The writer of Hebrews admonishes us not to neglect meeting "together, as is the habit of some, but encourag[e] one another, and all the more as you see the Day drawing near."[4]

The second thing Jude encouraged us to do is pray in the Holy Spirit. Romans 8:26 tells us how the Holy Spirit "helps us in our weakness. For we do not know what to pray for as we ought, but the Spirit himself intercedes for us with groaning too deep for words." Precious saint, when we are facing difficulties, when we can't even put two words together because we're so overwhelmed, we can speak in our heavenly language that we received from the Holy Spirit, and we can let Him intercede for us and through us. I'm reminded as well that Paul told the church at Ephesus to pray "at all times in the Spirit, with all prayer and supplication."[5] This is actually part of our weaponry, if you'll recall, that Paul listed for us. When we pray in the Holy Spirit, somehow our souls get encouraged, our spiritual fervor heats up, and we begin to come up out of the discouraged cave we've been living in.

The third thing Jude instructed us to do is of most importance, which is to keep in God's love. To do that, we need to come under the Iron Dome of authority.

UNDER THE IRON DOME OF AUTHORITY

Our hearts and affections are ultimately expressed in the form of worship. Satan knows that what God created you and me for was to enjoy God and to worship Him. And *the one thing that God wants more than anything out of you is your whole undivided heart, meaning your affections and your worship.* If Satan, however, can steal what God wants, he can put a breach in God's plans. *Remember, to Satan, your heart is the disputed territory of the battle.*

How do we keep our hearts connected to the love of God? We simply have to keep our lives under the authority of God. *Lawlessness is what produces cold hearts, remember? And lawlessness is living out from under God-ordained authority.* That leaves us open to attack because we have moved out from under the Iron Dome of God's protection. When we don't submit to God's authority, when we begin to do what's right in our own eyes, we start acting like our enemy. It's like we're switching camps.

There are two areas of authority that we need to submit our lives to on a regular basis. One is the authority of God's Word. God's Word remains forever. It is unchanging. It is unyielding. God spoke His Word into being, and it is resonating through the universe now, and it will forevermore. *We must submit our lives in every area to the authority and finality of God's Word.* And we haven't really submitted to God's Word until we've come to a place of disagreement with it. *Submission isn't submission until it starts with disagreement.* If you haven't read something in the Bible that you don't like, you haven't read the Bible long enough. Even so, it speaks the truth and does not lie. It knows what's best in all circumstances and situations. So, we would do well to submit to it so as to keep our hearts connected to the love of God.

The second place of spiritual authority that God has called us to submit ourselves to is to spiritual leadership. Now, talking about spiritual authority isn't popular because everybody points to the abuses of authority by some as a reason for the disqualification for all. And then there are many who try to say there is no such thing as spiritual authority other than God's because we're all equal children of His. Yes, we are all equal sons and daughters of God, but He has established spiritual authority—apostles, prophets, evangelists, pastors, and teachers—that protect us and that help equip us for ministry.[6]

Hebrews 13:17 provides us with some very good reasons to submit to spiritual authority. It says,

> Obey your leaders and submit to them, for they are keeping watch over your souls, as those who will have to give an account. Let them do this with joy and not with groaning, for that would be of no advantage to you.

We all need to have godly spiritual leaders in our lives. They provide love and counsel and encouragement and watchfulness. And all leaders need to be under another leader's authority so that they, too, are protected under God's Iron Dome, thus remaining connected to the love of God. The apostle Paul was an excellent example as a spiritual leader who was watchful and protective of the flock of God. He understood the enemy's constant attempts at a military coup of the Church.

APOSTOLIC ADVANCED DEFENSE SYSTEM

As a seasoned leader, the apostle Paul was aware of this major tactic of deception. It was something that concerned him when he was at the end of his third missionary journey, circling back to revisit the churches he had established on earlier trips. The church at Ephesus was one such church.

The Ephesian church met in multiple locations in the city of Ephesus, and it was a thriving, flourishing church at the time. It was one of the chief apostolic centers that Paul had founded. When Paul stopped in Miletus on his third trip, he called for the elders of Ephesus to meet him. Aware that this may be the last time he would be able to speak to these leaders he had trained and mentored, he sent word for them to travel the 50-mile journey from Ephesus to Miletus. His heart was set to encourage them and warn them of what he discerned could potentially harm the Ephesian flock of God. With passion, tears, and his heart wrapped around the elders, he said:

> And now, behold, I am going to Jerusalem, constrained by the Spirit, not knowing what will happen to me there, except that the Holy Spirit testifies to me in every city that imprisonment and afflictions await me. But I do not account my life of any value nor as precious to myself, if only I may finish my course and the ministry that I received from the Lord. . . . And now, behold, I know that none of you among whom I have gone about proclaiming the kingdom will see my face again. . . . Pay careful attention to yourselves and to all the flock, in which the Holy Spirit has made you overseers, to care for the church of God, which he obtained with his own blood. I know that after my departure fierce wolves will come in among you, not sparing the flock; and from among your own selves will arise men speaking twisted things, to draw away the disciples after them. Therefore be alert, remembering that for three years I did not cease night or day to admonish every one with tears. And now I

commend you to God and to the word of his grace, which is able to build you up and to give you the inheritance among all those who are sanctified.

ACTS 20:22–32

Paul warned the elders about several things in this passage. And the reason behind his admonishing them in this way was because Paul knew and understood a few things:

- He knew that what began pure can become tainted.
- He knew that what started powerfully can become weak over time.
- He knew that what originated in heaven can become hijacked by hell.
- And he knew that what God built in partnership with man's obedience can ultimately become corrupted and co-opted because of man's rebellion and Satan's deceptive influence.

How is it that something pure can become corrupted? How is it that something motivated by heaven can become fueled by hell? How is it that something powerful can become weak and powerless?

It all boils down to Satan's primary tactic of deception. *Deception undermines. Deception decays. Deception corrodes. It takes away the foundations and the footings.* And this was what the apostle Paul foresaw could happen after he would no longer be around to look out for the flock at Ephesus.

If we meditate on the text and try to picture it with our mind's eye in our day, Paul would be sitting with the elders around a conference table, pleading with them, "Leaders, you've got to keep this pure. You've got to keep Jesus as the main thing. You've got to listen to the Word of God. You've got to be leaders that pray." And we can see the elders looking at him and saying, "Paul, why are you so emotional about this? Look at the stat books. Look at the growth. Look at the salvations and baptisms. Look at what God's doing. Look at how the new locations are popping up all over the place in the city. We're overturning idols, and there's breakthrough and miracles. Why can't you just celebrate the victories?"

But in the back of Paul's mind, he knew that the enemy was not going to leave what God had started uncontested. He knew that, once he was no longer there, the enemy was going to work his way into the elders and the flock and even outsiders through cunning and deception. So, he warned them about falling prey to the enemy themselves, where instead of being shepherds who nurtured and cared for the flock of God, they acted like wolves dressed as sheep.

The King James Version translates, "Pay careful attention to yourselves," as "Take heed therefore unto yourselves."[7] What were they supposed to take heed about? That they were in the Faith. That they were paying attention to the state of their relationship with Jesus and were not succumbing to the deceptiveness of sin in selfish ambition or self-seeking. These elders needed other elders, other shepherds, who could pastor them. *True shepherds, good leaders, must have shepherds or leaders in their lives for accountability—to ask them the difficult questions and, like Paul, to warn and admonish them in their leadership.*

The job of a shepherd in a church is not to have his or her own voice, but it is to amplify the voice of the Good Shepherd, Jesus. And ultimately, it is to defend the flocks of God with their very lives. It is to pay careful attention to what's happening among the flock and what's happening in and around the flock. Wolves, on the other hand, are predators. They're false teachers or influencers that try to come in from the outside or rise up from the leadership within. And the Ephesian elders were admonished to beware of wolves, keep the sheep, feed the sheep, lead the sheep, and defend the sheep against the wolves.

Ignatius, one of the early Church Fathers, wrote in his memoirs that, although the church at Ephesus went through a season of decline in deception, because the leaders received these words of Paul prophetically spoken years earlier, they went into a season of prayer and fasting. The Ephesian church repented, and God renewed the lampstand of first love back to them. So, they adhered; they listened to the admonition of Paul. And so should we.

"Pay careful attention to yourselves and to all the flock." Don't be corrupted by the devil's deception. Stay pure. Stay watchful. Stay vigilant.

---

1. Revelation 12:9.
2. Matthew 24:10–12.
3. James 1:14–15.
4. Hebrews 10:25.
5. Ephesians 6:18.
6. See 1 Corinthians 12:27–31; Ephesians 4:10–12.
7. Acts 20:28 KJV.

NINE
CALIBRATING YOUR HEART'S CIRCADIAN RHYTHM

JESUS SAID the greatest challenge to Christians in this generation is not the external circumstances that are happening around us. It has everything to do with our inner lives, the preparation of our hearts within us. *We can't always control what is happening externally, but we do have control over what happens to us internally, meaning over our hearts and how we keep them.* Proverbs 4:23 (NKJV) says, "Keep [guard] your heart with all diligence, for out of it spring the issues of life." In a manner of speaking, this is what Jesus meant when He said, "Stay awake, take heed, watch and pray."

What did Jesus mean by telling us to stay awake? He wasn't necessarily talking about physically staying awake. He was referring to spiritual slumber that can overtake the lives of His most sincere and devout believers. Well acquainted with our humanity, Jesus knew that, as our environment grows darker, we tend to grow sleepier. It happens in both the natural and spiritual realms. If we aren't intentional about calibrating our hearts to the Kingdom of God, when darkness grows darker, we can succumb to spiritual slumber. I like to compare it to the effect daylight hours have on us Michiganlanders.

At the beginning of December, the sun goes down a little after 5:00 p.m. in Michigan's Eastern Time Zone. We have under nine and a half hours of daylight in early December. That leaves us with about fourteen and a half hours of darkness. Between the effects of the cold winter and the earlier sunsetting, many of us go to work when it is dark, we get out of work in the dark, and then we are ready to go home and get in our pajamas because it has been dark a long time. We ask ourselves, *How much longer do I have to stay awake? Not sure if I can, but if I go to bed this early, I'll be up at two-dark-thirty.*

By the time summer rolls around in July, however, we're getting three to four hours more of daylight, that many less hours of darkness, and we're enjoying warm temperatures. I mean, we're out in our backyards, grilling burgers and feeling wide awake as we try to squeeze in more life outside after 8:00 p.m. before it is too dark. We get tired later in the summer because it doesn't get dark until later.

DAYLIGHT VS. DARKNESS

According to Jesus, the Omega Generation will see the end-time signs and evil proliferate in ways that we would have never imagined. And the lines between those who love God and believe in His Word and those who love wickedness and call what's right wrong and what's wrong right will become more clearly delineated. A day is coming when it will be like Isaiah 60:2 (KJV) foretold, "For, behold, the darkness shall cover the earth, and gross darkness the people." *And what will happen to our souls as the darkness around us begins to get darker, quicker, sooner, and more intense is our spirits will come under the influence of a spirit of slumber, resulting in spiritual sleep and lethargy if we don't do something about it.* Thankfully, Jesus gave us the secret strategy to fight spiritual slumber: "Take heed, watch and pray." These three tactics will help calibrate our hearts to the time zone of heaven, the Kingdom of God. And *calibrating our hearts to the Kingdom of God will keep us from coming under the sway of the spirit of the age and its increasing darkness.*

Listen, we aren't in control of a lot of things, but we are in control of what happens in our own hearts. Nobody else is responsible for our hearts. They are ours to govern. We can submit our hearts to Jesus and His Kingdom, or we can submit our hearts by default to the spirit of this age. Because right now on the earth, there are two things that are at work: the Spirit of God and the spirit of this age.

The spirit of the age is a spirit of darkness. It is a spirit of heaviness or weightiness. Sin and evil, for instance, often produce an oppressive weight or heaviness on us. Sin is a burden, weight, or yoke. It can produce not only oppression, but depression in our lives, which can produce anxiety and fear.

The Spirit of God, however, is light. He's truth. He's revelation. He brings us into encounter with the Lord. He brings freedom to our hearts. The second half of Isaiah 60:2 says that, right during the gross darkness, "the Lord will arise upon [us], and his glory will be seen upon [us]." That's the light of God shining on us!

In God's economy, darkness is not the end. It is just the beginning. If we look back to Genesis 1:2, we read, "Darkness was over the face of the deep." But what is the first thing we read after that? God began His six days of creation. Verse 3 tells us the first thing He created was light. So, when God created everything, He called light out of darkness. He still calls light out of darkness. *Darkness is simply a setup for what God is going to do in these last days, which is to show forth His glory through His Church and people as we arise and shine.* That's what we see promised in Isaiah 60:2.

Additionally, the book of Romans says that the Kingdom of God is righteousness, peace, and joy in the Holy Spirit.[1] Do you know that you can have righteousness, peace, and joy in your life every single day regardless of how dark the world is becoming? It is because the Kingdom of God is within you. And you can submit yourself to the Kingdom of God. You can do what Jesus said in Matthew 6:34, "Do not be anxious about tomorrow, for tomorrow will be anxious for itself. Sufficient for the day is its own trouble."

Earlier in the same chapter, Jesus said not to worry about what you're going to wear or what you're going to eat.[2] Don't worry. Don't be anxious about anything. All the world—the *ethnos,* the Gentiles, the nations, the spirit of this world—is affected by worry and anxiety connected to tomorrow, but you are not called to live like the world. You are not called to live in sync with the world's time zone, where its darkness is psyching you out to think it is time to sleep. You are called to wakefulness—to "seek first the kingdom of God and his righteousness, and all these things [the things that you need] will be added to you."[3] *You need to align and calibrate your heart to the Kingdom of God, to the light of God, even though you are living in a grossly dark world.*

YOUR CIRCADIAN RHYTHM

Did you know that you have a circadian rhythm? It is the physical, mental, and behavioral changes you experience over a 24-

hour period or cycle. "Light and dark have the biggest influence on circadian rhythms, but food intake, stress, physical activity, social environment, and temperature also affect them."[4] Your brain falls into a pattern that then communicates to the rest of your body about activity or restfulness that is determined by the amount of light that is penetrating your eyes, hitting a cluster of nerves behind your eyes, which then communicates to your brain and either tells you it is time to stay awake when it is light, or it tells you it is time to go to sleep when it is dark. This is also known as *the sleep-wake cycle*.

So, you have a circadian rhythm, a pattern of sleep and wakefulness, that your body has gotten into. Most of us wake up sometime after sunrise and go to bed sometime after dark. If, however, you work a third-shift schedule, you may sleep during most of the day and stay awake all night. Any significant change, however, to one of the elements I mentioned earlier, like food intake or stress, can impact your circadian rhythm or sleep-wake cycle.

Traveling through multiple times zones can also impact your circadian rhythm. I remember when my wife, Jane, and I traveled to Hong Kong. Its time zone is thirteen hours ahead of the Eastern Time Zone. Any trip like that would probably give most people a real case of jet lag. You may find yourself sleeping during the daytime of the time zone you're visiting and staying up into the wee hours of the morning. The reason why you're wide awake is not because there's light. It is because your body is calibrated to a different time zone, and so you're wide awake because your body is calibrated to the time zone from which your trip originated. It takes one day per each time zone you crossed for you and your body and your sleep-wake cycle to get acclimated to the new time zone. So, if you stay someplace after a few days, you recalibrate to the new time zone. And then when you return home from your travels, your circadian rhythm will adjust back to the time zone you call home.

Why is this important to understand? Because, spiritually speaking, your home time zone is not Eastern, Central, Pacific, or Greenwich Time Zones. No, *your spiritual time zone is heaven and the Kingdom of God.*

SET TO HEAVEN'S TIME ZONE

The Bible says you and I are exiles. We're foreigners and strangers here on this earth. Philippians 3:20 says, "Our citizenship is in heaven, and from it we await a Savior, the Lord Jesus Christ." That means our home time zone should be set to heaven. *We should intentionally calibrate, align, sync our hearts to heaven, to the Kingdom of God.*

In Romans 13:11–14, the apostle Paul said:

Besides this you know *the time* [there it is], that *the hour* has come for you to *wake from sleep.* For salvation is nearer to us now than when we first believed. The *night* is far gone; the *day* is at hand. So then let us cast off the works of *darkness* and put on the armor of *light.* Let us walk properly as in the *daytime,* not in orgies and drunkenness, not in sexual immorality and sensuality, not in quarreling and jealousy. But put on the Lord Jesus Christ, and make no provision for the flesh, to gratify its desires [or passions].

According to the apostle, it is time for us to wake up. It is time for us to recognize that, even though it is dark outside in the world, there is a day that's dawning. *We have to align ourselves, not with the darkness, but with that day.* If we align ourselves with that day, we won't stumble or fall asleep because of the darkness outside. Paul explained in his first letter to the Thessalonians that we aren't children of the darkness, but children of the day. He wrote:

> For you are all *children of the light and of the day*; we don't belong to *darkness* and *night*. So be on your guard, not asleep like the others. Stay alert and be clearheaded. *Night* is the time when people sleep and drinkers get drunk. But let us who live in the *light* be clearheaded, protected by the armor of faith and love, wearing as our helmet the confidence of our salvation.
>
> 1 THESSALONIANS 5:5–8 NLT

In both Romans and 1 Thessalonians, Paul basically told us believers to wake up and calibrate our hearts to heaven's time zone so that the circadian rhythm of our hearts is in sync with our present and eternal home. *Whatever place your circadian rhythm is calibrated to is the place you have determined as your home.*

You see, when I travel overseas, if I stay there too long, I'll change my sleep-wake cycle, and I'll shift in my pattern of living. My eyes will start adjusting to the light and darkness there. So, while I'm away from home, I have to be intentional about staying connected to the time zone that I call home. That way, when I come back, it isn't too difficult to go on about my everyday life. I'm staying in my zone. But if I'm not intentional about staying in sync with my home time zone, I'll start to adjust and shift to the new time zone. That may be good for avoiding jet lag where I'm visiting, but it totally throws me off when I'm back home.

Christian, we are children of the light, children of the day. We are children of God's Kingdom, children of heaven. We cannot walk around in the darkness of this world and not have our hearts stay calibrated to our heavenly home. We're citizens of heaven, and we're promised a new day is dawning, and that means we must be intentional about the way we live our lives. If we don't, we'll begin to alter our lives, adjust to the darkness around us, and begin to fall asleep.

Have you ever noticed how you fall asleep? Really, really subtly. Nobody sits in a chair and goes, "All right, now it is sleep." No, you must get comfortable. I've got a whole thing that I have to do to go to sleep. It is rhythmic. I start on my side, then I go to my back. Next, I'll picture some beautiful, relaxing view. Why? Because my mind is constantly moving, the picture of that view in my mind helps me to stop thinking, rehearsing everything I did during the day. It makes me relax. The next thing I know, I'm waking up, and it is time for coffee. And Jane's like, "Alexa, turn on the coffee maker." And I'm like, "Ah, yes, here it comes." And you know what? I don't even remember having fallen asleep.

That's what can happen to us spiritually. We love Jesus. We love God. We want His Kingdom to come. We go to church, but as darkness begins to rise and manifest and get darker, we don't even realize it, but we're getting a little sleepy. "Yeah, yeah, yeah, yeah. No, I'm awake," our heads snap back, and our shocked eyes open wide. It reminds me of Jane. She always falls asleep when we sit down and watch a movie or TV show. Her falling asleep so quickly is a joke in our family. I'll look at her and catch her nodding off, and she'll say, "I'm watching. I'm awake." I'll turn around to pet the dog and look back at the screen. Then I'll quickly look at her, and I see her drifting, but she's like, "Oh, yeah, I totally know what's going on," as if she's feeling my eyes staring at her. But I know she doesn't know what's going on because she's slipping into sleep. Many times, she'll wake up forty or fifty minutes later and say, "What happened?" She missed the important stuff because she couldn't stay awake.

We don't want to be asleep when the greatest revival the world has ever seen takes place. We don't want to suddenly wake up after the fact and say, "Oh, what happened? What did I miss?" We don't want to wake up after Jesus has just returned, having spiritually slept through His arrival. *We cannot allow the influence of darkness to have more dominance in our lives than the light of the Spirit of the living God.*

The spirit of the age wants to lull us to sleep, wants us not to be prepared and ready for the Lord's return. *Beloved, the enemy wants your circadian rhythm to sync up with the darkness around you— even if it is just by default.* He wants to put you into his spiritual coma. He wants to get you to fall asleep because you've gotten drunk on the influence of this age. He wants you to become intoxicated on the spirit of the age. You can come under the influence of the spirit of the age, even through entertainment.

Do you know nothing will wear you out more spiritually than just getting bombarded with the same messages over and over? "This is right. This is right. This is right. This is how you live. This is what's important. This is what you're supposed to put your value on," and all the things the spirit of the age is saying are counter to the biblical truth and revelation of Jesus. The enemy just keeps bombarding you with them. He uses the media. He uses your friends. He uses situations. He uses your own imagination, and he just wears you down until you're asleep. Do you know that one of the descriptions in the book of

Daniel about how the antichrist will operate says he will wear out the saints? Daniel 7:25 says, the antichrist "shall speak words against the Most High, and shall wear out the saints of the Most High, and shall think to change the times and the law." If he can't convince you to reject God's Word or get you to adapt to the ideas and values of the cultural collective, and sear your conscience in one fell swoop, he'll just bombard you over, over, and over until one day you just fall asleep to truth—until one day you just don't even know it, but you've actually fallen into a spiritual coma, until one day you don't even realize you haven't heard the voice of God in months, until one day you look at your Bible and say, "I haven't read this in a year," until one day you find yourself in a relationship with somebody that will destroy your life. How did it happen? The same way you fall asleep. It happened without you realizing it because you adjusted your circadian rhythm to the darkness of this world rather than to the light of heaven and the Kingdom of God.

---

1. See Romans 14:17.
2. See Matthew 6:25.
3. Matthew 6:33.
4. "Circadian Rhythms," *NIH*, https://www.nigms.nih.gov/education/factsheets/Pages/circadian-rhythms.aspx/ (accessed January 17, 2024).

TEN
HOW TO STAY AWAKE

THERE WAS a righteous man who lived in one of two cities that God destroyed with fire and brimstone. That man's name was Lot, and he lived in Sodom. Speaking about him, the apostle Peter said Lot lived among the wicked "day after day," and Lot's soul was tormented over the "lawless deeds that he saw and heard."[1] The King James Version says Lot's soul was "vexed" by what he saw.

RESIST THE GRAVITATIONAL PULL

The wickedness of Sodom and Gomorrah is referred to numerous times in Scripture as the epitome of vile immorality and utter human depravity. In fact, Sodom was a byword.[2] What's interesting to note is Sodom was the place Lot selected to live when his relative Abraham gave him first choice of land. That day with Abraham, Lot had looked down into the Jordan Valley which was lush and green, and he had seen what he believed in the natural would be the key to his success and happiness.[3] "Thus they separated from each other. Abram settled in the land of Canaan."[4]

So, Lot moved into the valley near Sodom. But years later when God would judge Sodom for its wicked conduct, Lot no longer lived on the outskirts of the city, where the shepherds and herdsmen lived. Instead, he was living in the city proper.[5] You see, sin and the world and the devil have a gravitational pull. It is like a black hole. You get too close to that thing, and it will pull you down into it. That's what happens.

Day by day, every day by degree, we can calibrate to the time zone of the world, and day by day, our righteous souls can get tormented if we're not intentional in keeping our hearts calibrated to the Kingdom of God. *If we don't remind ourselves on a daily basis that we are children of the light, that we belong to the heavenly Kingdom, then we can slowly but surely acclimate to the darkness of this present age.* And like Lot, we don't even realize we're being pulled into the vortex of the world until we're vexed and tormented.

So as not to become like poor, righteous Lot who had to be extricated from Sodom by angelic hosts, we will have to act intentionally to stay awake and not be pulled or sucked into the darkness. Here are some other things we can do to stay awake.

DO NOT RELAX

If you are going to stay awake in these last days, you cannot relax. Now, I'm not saying don't find rest. You need to find rest, but your rest must be in God. Your rest is in His Word, in His peace, in His provision, in His love, and in His faithfulness. You cast your anxieties and cares upon Him.[6]

There is a difference, though, between resting in God and relaxing in the world. To relax means you let your guard down. To relax means you get comfortable. Like when you come home from a long, arduous day of work, you want to relax, to sit in your favorite, big, comfy chair. You put yourself in a position of comfort. You recline your seat and put up your feet. That's a picture of relaxing. But *we cannot relax in the world because that kind of relaxing means compromise. Compromise is cultural accommodation.* Compromise says *yes* to things that you know are less than the best for you. You compromise simply because it creates a false sense of ease. It is easier to go along to get along. When we say *yes* to compromise, however, we say *no* to consecration.

The Bible says every priest in the Old Testament who served in the temple had "a plate of pure gold" that was fastened on the front of his turban. It was engraved with these words, "Holy to the Lord."[7] That meant they were consecrated—set apart. We must be set apart as well. We are "a chosen generation, a royal priesthood, a holy nation, His own special people."[8] We are called to "be holy" because God is holy.[9] I'm not talking about legalism that's all caught up in doing works to get a pass from God. *Holiness is a condition of our hearts where we've consecrated or devoted ourselves to the Lord so that nothing comes between us and our relationship with Him—nothing separates us from intimacy with Him.* That's holiness.

Too many people are walking around and premeditating compromise. They're even using grace as some "get out of jail free" pass so that they can continue in sin. The apostle Paul handled that wrong thinking when he asked, "What shall we say then? Are we to continue in sin that grace may abound? By no means! How can we who died to sin still live in it?"[10] See, in a believer's life, compromise is a bacteria that breeds in comfort. It is a bacteria that breeds when you choose comfort over conviction, when you choose comfort over consecration. What you don't premeditate to set apart *for* God, remains open for the enemy to infect with temptation that leads to compromise. *The bacteria of compromise can fester into full-blown wickedness.*

Remember, before Jesus went to the cross, He said the god of this world was coming to tempt Him. Then He said that Satan had no place in or "claim on" Him.[11] Do you know why Satan had no place in Jesus? Because in every area of His life, He had put a wax seal that said, "Sanctified. Consecrated. This belongs to God. My identity, My success, what other people think of Me, My appetites, My desires, My dreams, My personal preferences—I've submitted them all to God. Satan, do not enter."

The areas that we do not submit to God, the areas where we're looking for comfort or something of this world to meet our personal needs, are areas open to temptation because they have not yet been sealed off. Neither has the "Do Not Enter" sign been posted, and the door is wide open. If you're going to stay awake in the last days, you can't relax. You must be wholly consecrated to the Lord.

STAY IN THE LIGHT

The second thing you should do to stay awake is stay in the light. *As long as you're in the light, your spirit will stay calibrated to the light.* The apostle John wrote, "If we walk in the light, as he is in the light, we have fellowship with one another, and the blood of Jesus his Son cleanses us from all sin."[12] God's desire for you is to walk in His light.

Psalm 119:105 says, "Your word is a lamp to my feet and a light to my path." That means every time we're taking God's

Word into our hearts as we read it, meditate on it, feed on it, and study it, we're exposing them to the light of the Kingdom of God. What's more is Jesus told His disciples the words He had spoken are "spirit and life."[13] He later told them that they were already "clean because of the word" He had spoken to them.[14] The Word of God cleanses and washes us.[15]

God's Word is powerful. It "is living and active, sharper than any two-edged sword, piercing to the division of soul and spirit."[16] Do you know the enemy deceives you when you can't tell the difference between what is a desire of your flesh or nature and what is the will of God for your life? In other words, what is spirit versus what is soul? That's another place where temptation can enter. We can follow our soulish natures rather than be led by the Spirit. But if we stay in the Word, it washes us, it lights our path, and we can calibrate our hearts to the light rather than calibrate them to the world, the flesh, or the devil.

Lot dealt with "all filthiness and rampant wickedness." That phrase appears in James 1:21, where James wrote to put away such things "and receive with meekness the implanted word, which is able to save your souls." James was not talking to people who were unsaved, so he wouldn't have been dealing with our accepting Christ as our Savior. What he was talking about is our souls or minds. Our brains want to calibrate to our flesh. Nature wants to immediately calibrate us to the world and to the darkness around us. This is where delusion and deception can enter, as we spoke about in chapter eight. And this is why James spoke of receiving the implanted Word with meekness or humility. The written Word is the mere reflection of the Living Word. As we are looking into the mirror of God's Word, we're seeing and we're beholding the image of His glory and of His will, and as that gets into us, it begins to change us.

Like seeds sown into the soil of our hearts, the implanting of His Word determines the root system and the fruit and what's growing out of our lives as we're exposed to the light.

If we sin or are confused, hurt, or offended, we tend to draw back from others, including God. We can step out of the light. When we do this, we're once again calibrating our hearts to darkness and are susceptible to deception and delusion. *The greatest thing you can do is to give your life to the Word and to stay in it each and every day. Expose yourself to daylight. Get it into your heart. The more light exposure, the more you have a framework of who God is and what His will is.* You begin to have a larger database of God's Word built up. The Holy Spirit will draw out the Word as we fellowship with Him.

Listen, every time you read the Word with a humble heart, you are in fellowship with Jesus. Every time you may not feel it, but you are. You can't come to the Word with meekness to receive it without the Holy Spirit coming and meeting you there. Meekness means I humble myself and I say God, "I'm coming to Your Word, and I'm saying to You that You're God, and I'm not. Your Word is Truth, and I submit to it." When we do that, the Word gets planted deep in our hearts, and it keeps us connected and calibrated to the light.

KEEP YOUR FOCUS

If you're going to stay awake, you must keep your focus. And to keep your focus requires you to stay alert. To stay alert, you have to give yourself something to do so your mind doesn't wander, you don't get distracted, or you don't nod off to sleep. The second you let your mind go idle, your alertness is gone as is your focus. In these last days, you've got to stay focused.

We looked at Romans 13:11–14 in the last chapter when we were talking calibrating our circadian rhythm to the time zone of heaven. We know from these verses in Romans 13 that Paul was letting the believers know it was time to wake up. It was time for daytime living. He referred to the sexual immorality and debauchery that was dominant in the Roman culture and time. In fact, business was behind the perversions of the day, very much like what we have going on in our culture. It's nothing new. It has been around for a long time because the human mind in its depraved state can always twist, pervert, and create an appetite for something that's more and more twisted. The believers in Rome that Paul was writing to got saved out of that. But the problem was these believers had to live in that culture. Some may have had jobs requiring them to go to the marketplace or the bath houses within the gymnasiums. The prostitutes were also there, and everything sexual was all wrapped up together. So, many of the Roman Christians were getting pulled back into the perversity of the Roman culture.

Paul, however, was telling the believers not to get wrapped up in all the sexual immorality of the culture. The defense against that was to "put on the Lord Jesus Christ"—the Light of the world.[17] It was like putting on the armor of light. In other words, defend yourself with God's light, with His standards, with His Word.

Paul told them not to give room to compromise in the flesh in any way. What would that require? Focus. It would require intentional focus on what to do and what not to do. If they didn't keep their focus, if they didn't stay alert, the enemy would take over by default. And this is what we're seeing happen in the last days right before our eyes. Many people who have claimed to be followers of Jesus have compromised themselves in the immorality of our culture. Oftentimes, when Paul talked about falling away in compromise, it led to a sexual immorality issue.

In the Old Testament, sex and idolatry went hand in hand. The worship of the idols in a culture was always fully expressed in sexuality. Why? It is because our bodies were actually created to worship God. In Romans 12:1 (NKJV), Paul entreated, "I beseech you, therefore, brethren, by the mercies of God, that you present your bodies a living sacrifice, holy, acceptable to God, which is your reasonable service." So here's what our Christian culture believes today—that we can live immorally and still love Jesus. But that is utter deception, and if "believers" keep espousing to this way of living and thinking, it will lead to delusion. *Our bodies are for worship, for living surrendered to the will and purposes of God. Our bodies are not to be offered on the altars of our culture or on the altars we've made to ourselves.*

You'll notice, in our day and age, even in the Church, major denominations are splitting over the issue of sexual ethics. Why is that? It is because the enemy wants to pervert the worship of God by perverting the Body of Christ. Satan wants to take the members of Christ's Body that are in spiritual union with Christ, and Satan wants to pervert them, twist them, because he hates Jesus and because he wants to steal all the honor and glory and worship from Jesus.

What we need is a return to sanctification, where our bodies are living sacrifices to Jesus—to where our bodies are sacred. What I do with my body matters. Second Corinthians 5:10 says that we will all stand before Christ and give an account for what we did with our bodies. *Our bodies are sacred. Our bodies are the temple of God.*[18] Living in our sexually immoral culture requires alertness, focus, and intentionality.

Beloved, stay in the light and keep your focus so you don't get blind-sided. What you don't focus on becomes a blindside, and the enemy most often works in the arena of temptation and deception in your peripheral vision, not in the thing you're focused on. If you've ever sat in your house and seen a mouse run across the room in your peripheral vision, you don't know it is a mouse. You're like, "I just saw something move. What was that?" That's how the enemy works. He runs and works in the peripheral, in your blindside. So, you must stay alert and focused.

STAY FUELED

What do we need in this hour? We need God's Presence. What do we need in this hour to turn the tide? We need the oil of intimacy with Jesus, with the One who is returning at the most critical time in human history. We need to buy oil from Him.

In Matthew 25:1–13, Jesus used a parable that analogized what the Kingdom of God will be like at the end of the age. He compared it to ten virgins who were going out to meet the bridegroom. Five were wise in that they took extra oil with them and had prepared their lamps for use. The other five were foolish in that they had no extra oil with them and their lamps were unprepared.

As the bridegroom was delayed, Matthew 25:5 says all ten virgins "became drowsy and slept." But someone was watching because "at midnight there was a cry, 'Here is the bridegroom! Come out to meet him.' Then all those virgins rose and trimmed their lamps."[19] But the five foolish virgins ran out of oil. And the five who were unwise said to the five who were wise, "Hey, give us some of your oil." The wise virgins refused to share their oil because they then wouldn't have enough for themselves. So, the foolish five went to buy oil, but when they returned to enter the marriage feast and see the bridegroom, it was too late. The door was shut. Unlike the wise five, the foolish five missed the bridegroom's return. Jesus then ended the parable with these words, "Watch therefore, for you know neither the day nor the hour."[20]

Oil is a picture of intimacy with the Lord. In essence, *Jesus was saying the rarest commodity in the Church or among His people at the end of the age is going to be the oil of intimacy that goes the distance.* It is going to be the oil—the all-consuming fire of intimacy and vulnerability with Jesus—that will keep us from spiritual coldness. The rarest commodity is not going to be platinum or some rare mineral. It isn't going to be gold. It isn't going to be oil for our cars. It is going to be the oil of intimacy that we have with the Lord, and only those who have that oil of intimacy will be able to go the distance because there's going to be so many things that are going to try and drive us back into hiding like Gideon.

You see, intimacy produces courage, and courage is one of the things we will need to be able to stand the test of time in the darkest hour. You and I will need fuel to maintain light and strength in the growing darkness. And as the parable shows us, *there's no such thing as secondhand intimacy. You can't borrow somebody else's oil of intimacy. You have to have your own.* You have to secure it beforehand. You have to purchase it, which means you have to pay a price or even sacrifice for it.

You can't stay awake if you don't have oil. You will fall asleep if you do not have a fresh flow of the oil of intimacy with Jesus. It is just a reality. You will fall asleep when the Master is delayed, when it gets darker than you thought it was going to get, when it takes longer than you thought it was going to take and you didn't prepare. Without the light, without the oil, you will grow sleepy. Your eyes will try to adjust to the darkness rather than the light.

In John 15, Jesus spoke about abiding in Him. He said He is the vine, and we are the branches.[21] The branches must abide in the vine because that's where life is. No life exists for us apart from our abiding in intimacy with Him. If we get disconnected from the vine, we don't bear fruit. If we get disconnected from the vine, the life and the sap that are in the vine don't flow into our lives. Therefore, we must abide in Christ, we must fellowship with Him and His Word, and we must maintain that connection because it is where we get our oil of intimacy.

Listen, the relationship between a husband and a wife, provides a great illustration of the relationship between Christ and the Church. In Ephesians 5:32 (NKJV), Paul spoke of that relationship as "a great mystery." Yet the best way to illustrate the relationship was to compare it to marriage, thereby instructing wives and husbands how to live and love together while seeing what God intended for the Bridegroom and His Bride. If we go back then, and we look at what God said about marriage, we'll find a master key to how we are to relate to Jesus.

First in Genesis 2:21–22, God took a rib from Adam and made woman from it. He created Eve, Adam's bride, from Adam's side. Where did God create the Church from? From the blood that flowed from Jesus' side. We, then, are His Bride that's being prepared for Him. Genesis 2:24 says, "Therefore a man shall leave his father and his mother and hold fast [or cleave] to his wife, and they shall become one flesh." In other words, everything that we had and everything that we viewed as security, identity, provision, we leave that behind. That's mother and father, and that's the world. The Church must do likewise as Jesus is her Husband. We must cleave to Him, holding on to Him for dear life. That's intimacy! *Cleaving is the master key to intimacy.*

We must recognize that we can't borrow oil from other people. You and I must have our own history with Jesus. That's the hardest thing to do, I think, to train people as disciples to stop thinking in short-term realities and start thinking in long-term history. Everybody wants a *bam* moment. We want to be slain in the Spirit. We want to be hit by the power of God or be overwhelmed in some marvelous encounter. We want to be in a worship service where the glory of God comes in like a tidal wave, washes over us, and we're never the same again. And I'm grateful for encounter moments like the ones I mentioned. They're powerful. But that's not where change happens. *Change happens every day. It happens when you're drawing near to Him, when you're fighting the gravitational pull away from Him, when you're cleaving to Him in desperation for life.* If we only come to Jesus because we want the glam shot, or we want the big event or the newest and coolest, big-hype thing, then we will be disappointed and fall away. The good news is Jesus is in it for the long haul with us. You're never going to shock Jesus with your weakness. He's never going to look at you and say, like some young, inexperienced bridegroom, "I didn't know that about you, so I guess I don't love you now. We should call it quits." Jesus is in it for everything and forever. He wants to prepare us as His Bride for the great wedding day that's coming.

Beloved, you need the oil of intimacy. You need fuel for the journey ahead. It will keep the light on. It will keep you calibrated with the Kingdom of God. It will help you stay awake.

NEVER TRAVEL ALONE

If you want to stay awake during the darkness of the hour, you must never travel alone. There is a reason Jesus sent His disciples out two by two. It was wise to do, for as Solomon wrote:

> Two are better than one, because they have a good reward for their toil. For if they fall, one will lift up his fellow. But woe to him who is alone when he falls and has not another to lift him up! Again, if two lie together, they keep warm, but how can one keep warm alone? And though a man might prevail against one who is alone, two will withstand him—a threefold cord is not quickly broken.
>
> ECCLESIASTES 4:9–12

You and a fellow Christian traveler can journey together more successfully than you can individually. You can cheer up each other, help up each other, and back up each other.

Hebrews 10:24–25 (NKJV) provides an eschatological reason for not traveling alone:

> And let us consider one another in order to stir up love and good works, not forsaking the assembling of ourselves together, as is the manner of some, but exhorting one another, and so much the more as you see the Day approaching.

The writer was saying that, *as the Day of the Lord comes closer, we in the Body of Christ need each other more, not less. We need to spend more time together, not less.* Why? Because there's strength when we're together. Because we can stir each other up to love and to do good deeds. Because there's vulnerability when we're isolated.

One of the things I watched during the pandemic of 2020 was how some people flourished as they still found ways to gather together and pull together. These recognized the urgency of the hour and didn't draw away from others. Then, I noticed people who isolated themselves. These pulled away from others, they withdrew from their churches, and they were harmed by it. Some became depressed, and others grew bitter, allowing the grief that resulted from loss of loved ones and friends to turn to anger against God and His people. A lot of people deconstructed and walked away, departed from the Faith in 2020. They got addicted to porn. They got overwhelmed with anxiety and depression. They took on substances. They began to experiment with other religions, other faiths, reading some things they probably had no business reading. It vexed their righteous souls.

We should never travel alone because we need each other for a safe journey to our destination. In ancient times, they traveled in caravans with more than two people. When somebody became isolated, they became vulnerable to robbers. Our enemy is a robber. He's a thief. You know what a thief and a con man are looking for? They're looking for a vulnerable person, an isolated individual. This is why we never, ever, travel through life alone. We need comrades, we need brothers and sisters, we need mothers and fathers, and we need the corporate gathering. *We need to be together more and more as the Day approaches because there's safety in those numbers.*

I'm reminded of the flying V-formation that geese use as they migrate. Their formation is aerodynamic. The geese take turns being the lead goose and the point of the V. And they honk at each other to communicate. They can fly much farther together than they can fly alone because of their rotation and the aerodynamic form they make. But I see that honking as being similar to what Hebrews 10:25 says we should do, and that is exhort one another.

Exhort is a military command. It isn't just encouragement. It is calling people out. Think of boot camp, where your drill sergeant or fellow soldier is verbally provoking you to perform, to push forward, to press on. *The exhortation is meant to get you to go farther than you've gone before on your own. That's exhortation. It is pushing you beyond what you think you're capable of and is giving you strength.*

Never travel alone. You and I need the help of exhortation, the kindness of friends.

DON'T LAY DOWN

Finally, how do you stay awake? You don't lay down. You just keep moving. When you stop moving, when you stop making progress, that's when you can fall asleep. What's the opposite of laying down? It is standing up. We must keep standing.

The Bible says in Ephesians 6:13 (NKJV), "Therefore take up the whole armor of God, that you may be able to withstand in the evil day, and having done all, to stand." When Roman sentries stood as watchmen, they stood the entire time. They never sat down. The same thing goes for posted guards today on a military citadel. They stand the entire time and never sit down. And in formal troop formation, troops never sit down. *Standing is a posture of readiness.*

The apostle Paul taught the Ephesians to put on the armor of God with the sole purpose of helping them learn how to stand. As we discussed in chapter five, Paul reviewed the weaponry and armor that is available to us believers. It was after he listed these things in Ephesians 6 that he basically said, "Put on this armor so that you are prepared as a soldier to face the evil day, and do everything you can to stand—then stand!"

Soldier, we are living in the evil day. We need to be able to stand, and how we do that is we put on the full armor of God. This is essential for us. We put on the helmet of salvation, the breastplate of righteousness, the shield of faith, the belt of truth, and the preparation of the gospel of peace on our feet. We wield the sword of the Spirit. We stand awake, alert, and aware. We take heed, watch, and pray in evil day.

———————————————

1. 2 Peter 2:6–8.
2. See Ezekiel 16:56.
3. See Genesis 13:10–12.
4. Genesis 13:11–12.
5. See Genesis 19:1–2.
6. See 1 Peter 5:7.
7. Exodus 28:36–37.
8. 1 Peter 2:9 NKJV.
9. 1 Peter 1:15–16.
10. Romans 6:1–2.
11. John 14:30.
12. 1 John 1:7.
13. John 6:63.
14. John 15:3.
15. See Ephesians 5:26.
16. Hebrews 4:12.
17. Romans 13:14.
18. See 1 Corinthians 6:19.
19. Matthew 25:6–7.
20. Matthew 25:13.
21. See John 15:5.

ELEVEN
TAKE HEED TO YOURSELF

WHEN JESUS TOLD His disciples to "take heed," He was talking about their keeping themselves free from deception. The phrase *take heed* means *to beware*. In other words, if you aren't paying attention, something bad can happen. *And when it comes to the enemy's tactic of using deception, you need to understand that he is looking to get an inroad into your life that will take you farther than you want to go, keep you somewhere longer than you want to stay, and cost you more than you want to pay.* He will start off small, but he will set you on a trajectory that, when you arrive at his destination for you, it won't be life. It will be destruction.

LOOK IN THE MIRROR

As I've mentioned before, this weapon the enemy unleashes in the last days is a weapon of mass destruction, and I've said that because there's going to be mass deception that takes place. A specific time will come "when people will not endure sound teaching, but having itching ears they will accumulate for them-selves teachers to suit their own passions, and will turn away from listening to the truth and wander off into myths."[1]

Why will people get deceived in the last days? Because they aren't paying attention to the truth. They aren't guarding their hearts. They aren't staying submitted to spiritual authority. They only listen to people who say things that they want to hear or things that line up with their own desires. As a result, they will be more interested in what's happening outside—what they hear and see happening around them—instead of paying atten-tion to their own hearts and what's happening inside them.

More than ever before, we need to guard our hearts from error and false teaching. *We must be in the Word, looking into the spiritual mirror of the Word, to let it offer us a truthful appraisal or eval-uation of our hearts and lives.* That's why Jesus said, "Take heed."

When we look in the mirror of God's Word, we should ask ourselves searching questions like:

- Am I staying in the Faith?
- Am I walking closely with the Lord?
- Are there sins in my life that I'm not dealing with?
- Are there motivations in my heart that the Holy Spirit is confronting me about and asking me to place at the foot of the cross?
- Are there things that are irritating me, or people for that matter, that I'm not bringing to Jesus and asking Him to forgive me for my attitude and frustration?
- Are there things that I'm reading in the Scriptures that I'm not doing because I just don't think I need to —things I think I can get a pass on?
- Am I loving God and others well?

- Am I living a surrendered and an obedient life, or am I doing my own thing?

Taking heed is about looking in a mirror spiritually and submitting that to God. It is saying, "God, I've got to take care of me lest I become deceived." I think Paul said it best when he said, "Therefore let anyone who thinks that he stands take heed lest he fall."[2]

A SEARED CONSCIENCE

Friend, there is a demonic war going on, and your heart is the war prize. Seducing spirits are trying to snipe you. Doctrines of demons are trying to convince you. And if these are successful, it will result in the searing of your conscience.[3] What that means is your heart won't be able to feel anymore. The thought of that should wake you up now before it is too late.

You see, nobody wakes up in the morning in the middle of the last days amid the persecution and crazy chaos that's going on and says, "Today, I'm going to choose to be deceived. Today, I'm going to let down my guard. Today, I'm going to invite the enemy's lies to seduce me, to deceive me to the point where I begin to live a hypocritical life—so much so that as the Holy Spirit is speaking and drawing me back to Jesus, I'm still living my life distracted by everything that's going on in this world. I'm paying attention to what everybody else is saying. I'm going to choose to be offended by what I'm witnessing around me, and I'm going to refuse to listen to the Holy Spirit anymore. I'm going to stop reading the Bible."

That's not what happens. That's not reality. Instead, what happens is the subtlety and stealth of the seducing spirits and demonic doctrines, along with the many distractions of life, make us less self-aware, less heedful, and more vulnerable.

I feel the weight and the sobriety of the hour we're living in because, as a pastor, I see people not realize they're caught in deception. I'm a shepherd of a large flock, and I see people drifting away and falling prey to the adversary, even after much warning by me, their friends, and their families. I've been pastoring the same wonderful church for twenty-seven years,[4] I've spoken at churches across the US, and what I've noticed is how many individuals are coming under deception or offense that makes them shut down. I know people over the last several years, people who loved Jesus with all of their hearts a decade ago, now say, "I don't even believe in Jesus anymore." They've become wrapped up in ideologies and -isms and have sold out their souls to such things. And I'm afraid the consciences of some of them have been seared because they seem lifeless, like dead men walking without hope.

I've learned I shouldn't stand in judgment of these individuals, nor say something like, "I can't believe that they did that. I can't believe they didn't listen and heed the warnings." No, Jesus calls me to take heed to myself. And Jesus calls you to do the same. He says to us today, "Don't think you're above this—as if it could never happen to you. You, too, could become deceived. Don't withdraw from My Presence or My Word. Don't pull away from fellowship with Me or other believers. Beware and pay attention. Take heed, watch, and pray."

THE DEVIL'S AIM

The devil's goal in deceiving us isn't just random. He is aiming to accomplish something. *He wants to steal our authority that's connected to our God-given mission. If he can accomplish that, then he can prevent you and me from living on mission.*

At the end of Mark 13, Jesus compared His return to "a man going to a far country, who left his house and gave authority to his servants, and to each his work."[5] In other words, Jesus was talking about the delegated authority and mission He gave to His Church. We're His followers. We're His *doulos,* which is a Greek word meaning *bondservants.* He gave us authority and some Kingdom work to do. What's our Kingdom work? To preach the gospel, to make His name famous, to make Him known to those who are far from Him, to live gospel-centric lives.

What does deception do? *Deception stupefies and disarms us so that we lose our authority.* There is a pattern of this that goes all the way back to Genesis 1–3. In Genesis 1:26, God said, "Let us make man in our image, after our likeness." Then we read in the next verse in the New King James Version, which says, "Male and female He created them." And in verse 28, He said, "Be fruitful and multiply and fill the earth and subdue it." So man was created to be image bearers of God in the earth. God gave us delegated authority over the entire planet, and He told us to go out and subdue it and bring it under dominion.

But then the enemy entered Eden. What did the enemy do when he found Eve alone in the garden? He said, "Did God actually say?"[6] He immediately challenged God's word. Eve tried to explain that she was told not to eat of the tree and that, if she did eat, she would die. Then he lied in response and said, "You will not surely die. For God knows that when you eat of it your eyes will be opened, and you will be like God, knowing good and evil."[7] And what did Satan do? He played on Eve's desire because she saw the fruit of the tree that she wasn't supposed to eat and thought it looked good and delightful.[8] Therefore, she wanted it. Deceived, Eve ate the fruit and then shared it with Adam, and he ate it as well.[9]

I always look at this part of the story and think of how Adam could have prevented the deception or at least helped Eve repent after she ate the forbidden fruit. What should Adam have done? Adam should have said, "What have you done, Eve? We must tell God and ask Him for mercy." He should have taken his place as her husband and lovingly used his authority to go with her before the Father and repent, "Father, Eve ate of the fruit. Satan tempted her. I didn't eat of it when she offered it to me, but she is bone of my bone and flesh of my flesh, and we repent of this." But no, instead, he took what Eve gave him and ate it, too. Why? Because of pressure. He didn't want to be left out. He didn't want to be the only one standing, and the enemy stole their authority by deception.

Beloved, if you are a follower of Jesus, you have authority. Jesus has given it to you. Remember what Jesus told His disciples? He said, "I have given you authority to tread on serpents and scorpions, and over all the power of the enemy, and nothing shall hurt you."[10] As disciples of Jesus Christ, you and I have authority over the enemy and his demons. In Matthew 28:18, when Jesus was about to ascend into the heavens, He told His disciples, "All authority in heaven and on earth has been given to me," and then He said, "Go therefore and make disciples of all the nations," right in the next verse. What was He giving them? Authority—authority to go and make disciples.

Christian, the enemy can only steal your authority if he can deceive you. But if he can't deceive you, he can't disarm you of your God-given authority over him. If you allow him to deceive you, however, you'll be left dumbfounded and confused—unable to bring your vision into focus—and you won't fulfill your mission. When Jesus comes back, or we see Jesus after our death or resurrection, we don't want to be those who are standing before Him empty-headed or empty-handed, saying, "Jesus, You sent me to this planet to preach the gospel, to live my life, to go to my job, to be salt and light to my friends and my family and my neighbors, to be an example of what it means to be saved and redeemed by Your blood. But yet I squandered that because I got deceived. I got deceived into thinking that this world was my home. I got deceived into thinking it was all about me. What I wanted—the fruit that was hanging on the tree of the knowledge of good and evil that I wanted for myself, my decisions, and my pursuit—gave the enemy permission to come in and deceive me and seduce me. That's what he does. He's so seductive, and, Jesus, I'm sorry, but I don't have anything, not even any fruit, to give You."

Deception comes in our lives—this is important—by what we give authority to. That's how deception shows up. It comes by what we give authority to in our lives, to whom we choose to listen or what we choose to follow. So, if we're paying attention, if we have voices in our lives that, when they speak, we listen, they now have authority in our lives. If there's a teacher, and we take what that teacher says as truth, then we have now opened the door and given the teacher authority over our lives. Just like Adam and Eve, they chose to believe the deceiver instead of God. And what did they do? They gave authority to him. So whatever or whoever it is in your life—listen to me, saint—that you are choosing to believe or to come under, you give authority over your life to that thing or person. The Bible uses the word picture of leaven to talk about this idea of giving our authority to someone and how that affects us.

BEWARE OF LEAVEN

When talking about leaven, the best thing to compare it to in our day is yeast. When you make bread, you use a leavening agent called *yeast*. Jesus used leaven as a word picture of the Kingdom of God in Matthew 13:33 to convey its capacity to thoroughly influence everything around it. But Jesus also used three types of leaven that are influences we need to beware of. He told us to:

- Take heed and beware of the leaven of the Pharisees.[11]
- Take heed and beware of the leaven of the Sadducees.[12]
- Take heed and beware of the leaven of Herod.[13]

In my estimation, these are the three most dangerous areas in which believers get deceived and offended, and our hearts begin to grow cold toward Jesus as a result. The enemy deceives believers through leaven because here's how leaven works. You put leaven in, and you don't hear it. Nobody hears it. It doesn't make a sound. It is subtle. When you put leaven into the dough, the leaven takes over the whole thing over the course of time. And if you watch it in time lapse sped up, you can see it happening. But if you watch it in real time, it is so slow that you don't see anything happening. That's how spiritual deception happens. This is some dangerous stuff!

Now, the first leaven Jesus told us to beware of—to take heed of—was the leaven of the Pharisees, which refers to the spiritual influence of the Pharisees. *The leaven of the Pharisees is the lie or the deception that you can have a relationship with God based on your performance and not by grace.* That's what the Pharisee did.

He said, "I keep the law more than anybody else, and so I perform, and I do good things and righteous things. And because of that, God loves me." What's the truth of grace? Well, God loves me, and, therefore, I do good things, but I don't gain God's love by doing good things. The Pharisees thought they were righteous and holy by the good works that they lived. We call this *legalism,* and I've seen many Christians get wrapped up in this. "I want to prove to God how righteous I am. I'm better than other people, and I'm going to make God love me and approve me." And so they're grinding it out, doing the right things in order to gain God's approval. My friend, that is deception. *You were created for good works, but you were created for good works that were empowered by grace, not a highway to get God's grace.*[14] Using your good works to gain God's love is the leaven of the Pharisees.

The leaven of the Sadducees refers to their spiritual influence. *The Sadducees didn't believe in angels or the resurrection. They didn't believe in the supernatural. They didn't believe in demons. Theirs was an intellectual, anti-supernatural spirituality that was nothing but empty ritual.* The leaven of the Sadducees is intellectualism that says, "I can know God, and I can be right with God through the acts of intellectualism. I just have an anti-supernatural bias." What does this leaven produce in us? Arrogance and compromise.

So many people begin loving Jesus, passionately reading their Bibles, and then they begin to read something that calls the Bible into question, calls Jesus into question. It leads them to think maybe He's not the only way, or maybe He's one of many different ways. And they get hung up on intellectual offenses. What they do, then, is they separate themselves, and they begin to go down the path of an intellectual, almost a secular, Christianity, where they begin to just become very liberal in their approach. What happens next is their love for Jesus doesn't increase. It just decreases. This is what the Sadducees did. They became arrogant and compromising. "Well, you know what? I think you can live sexually any way that you want to because the Bible was written 2,000 years ago. It doesn't really apply to us anyway. The Bible's not inspired. It contains some of God's ideas, but not all of God's ideas." Who told you that? "Well, I read this book by a PhD." That's what happens when you allow the leaven of the Sadducees in your life.

The leaven of Herod was the third type of leaven Jesus warned us about. Who was Herod? Herod was a puppet king that the Romans installed as the king of the Jews so that the Jews felt like they had a king. However, Herod was actually a king the Romans could partner with to keep the Jewish people in check. *The leaven of Herod is the political spirit. It is where Christians begin to look at political alignment as the means to accomplish what only the gospel can.* And in election years, we see this a lot. I believe it sickens Jesus. We act as if Jesus aligns Himself with a certain political party. Listen, He doesn't work that way. He is God. We either align with Him, or we don't. He is not obligated to side with our political party.

Can I just tell you church history is replete with 2,000 years of Christendom trying to do that very thing, and some of the worst moments for the Church in history took place when the Church went from being persecuted to having political power and sway. There have been those Christian leaders who have been tempted by people of power in politics to throw their proverbial hat in the ring. Such political powerhouses have offered to put Christian leaders in seats of authority to secure votes for their own agendas. "Come on, we'll give you some power. Just vote the way we want you to on this bill. Make sure you get behind this piece of legislation for us," they're told. I'm not saying we shouldn't be a prophetic voice in our generation or shouldn't be involved in affecting the affairs of our country, but we should not be an echo of or rubber stamp to someone else's political agenda. And the leaven of Herod is seductive to the Church. *We need to proclaim one King. We need to hold all political powers and authorities to the standard of the Word of God, and we need to beware of the leaven of Herod.*

In these last days, our energy and passion should be given to the proclamation of the gospel. If we come under the influence of any one of these three types of leaven, our lives will be spent on other things. Yet what we are supposed to live for as His Church is for His glory and for making Him known to the lost. It doesn't mean that we're not engaged in our world. Quite the opposite, we are carriers of His Kingdom wherever we go. We bring the leaven of the Kingdom of God with us, knowing His Kingdom is advancing and expanding. Our one true allegiance belongs to One, our King Jesus. When Jesus comes back, He isn't running for office. He has already won the throne. In the meantime, let's work like the Master of the house is coming back. Let's stay awake. He could come at any moment. Let's walk in our authority that Jesus gave us, let's fulfill our mission, and let's take heed to ourselves.

---

1. 2 Timothy 4:3–4.
2. 1 Corinthians 10:12.
3. 1 Timothy 4:2.
4. My wife, Jane, and I started Radiant Church in 1996. I've pastored Radiant for twenty-seven years at the time this book was published (2024).
5. Mark 13:34 NKJV.
6. Genesis 3:1.

7. Genesis 3:4–5.
8. See Genesis 3:6.
9. See 2 Corinthians 11:3.
10. Luke 10:19.
11. Matthew 16:6.
12. Ibid.
13. Mark 8:15.
14. See Ephesians 2:8–10.

TWELVE
WATCH: THE CALL TO
THE WALL

IN THE FIRST CENTURY, at the very beginning of the Church, there was great anticipation that the return of the Lord was going to take place quickly. Though Jesus had told them no one knew the day of His return except the Father, the early believers thought it would be very soon. We can deduce this from the Epistles as we see a real sense of urgency arise in the apostolic message. And we know from history that their pressing perception of the Lord's soon return greatly impacted how they and their fellow believers lived their daily lives.

Beloved, we should have an even greater sense of urgency since many of the signs Jesus forewarned us about and the game-changing signs we discussed in previous chapters are happening or have happened. Can you hear the heavenly trumpet sounding revelry? It is calling us to wakefulness. It is calling us to watchfulness. The words of Paul are resounding today: "The hour has come for you to wake from sleep. For salvation is nearer to us now than when we first believed."[1]

In my mind's eye, I can see God's people everywhere, jumping out of our army cots, getting dressed in our army fatigues and armor, lacing up our combat boots, grabbing our gear, guns, and ammo, and running to our positions on the wall. There we wait. And there we watch.

WATCH! WATCH! WATCH! WATCH! WATCH!

In the New King James Version's rendering of Mark 13, the word *watch* appears five times.[2] The same Greek word was not used for each of the five times, but three synonyms were employed to convey this military idea of standing watch like a guard or sentinel.[3] That's why in different versions we read phrases like "stay alert," "be on your guard," "stay awake," "be on alert," or "take heed" where the New King James uses "watch."

What we need to realize from this is just how impacting Jesus meant for this message to be to His disciples. If Jesus had used the military jargon of our day to tell His disciples to watch, it could have sounded something like this: "Watch! Attention! Watch! Standby to standby! Watch! Full battle rattle! Watch! Check your six! Watch! Incoming!" Hear the urgency? *Jesus desired His disciples to perceive the critical hour they were in. He wanted them to understand watching was a matter of life and death.*

You see, here's the problem with not recognizing the urgency of the time or situation. You set yourself up for possible harm. To stick with the military imagery, imagine being in the army and posted to a watch. You're supposed to be surveilling the enemy under the dark of night. You have your infrared, night vision goggles on. You're hidden high above the enemy's camp, and you're looking for any and all movement. You can't afford to fall asleep. You can't afford to be lazy or purposely disengage in the watch. You can't afford to be negligent. Why? Because if you're remiss in any way to maintain your watch, some destructive attack or calamity can suddenly befall you or those you were supposed to be protecting or looking out for.

Soldier, we must watch. We cannot afford to fall asleep in this hour. Wakefulness is watchfulness. And Jesus wants us to be watchful. Ultimately, His disciples got the message, but it wasn't until after they fell asleep at a critical hour.

"WILL YOU NOT WATCH WITH ME?"

Having shared their last Passover meal together, Jesus and His disciples left the Upper Room in the evening and made their way to the Garden of Gethsemane on the Mount of Olives. They often went to the garden, resting under the evergreen olive trees. The name *Gethsemane, Gat Shemanim* in Aramaic, means *olive press*, indicating the presence of an ancient olive oil mill. This was recently confirmed as archeologists unearthed a 2,000-year-old *Mikveh*, a ritual bath, in the Gethsemane area which they said "confirm[ed] the ancient name of the place" as this would have been where workers involved in oil making during Jesus' day would have taken their ritual baths.[4]

Very soon, Jesus would be facing betrayal at the hands of one of His disciples. Judas would lead others to Jesus and with a kiss identify Jesus as the one to be arrested. Jesus knew the cross was coming. He understood His death was rapidly approaching, and He was prophetically aware what His friends, His disciples, were about to face. He had even warned them in His conversations with them. For example, He told Peter as they left the Upper Room, "Truly, I tell you, this very night, before the rooster crows, you will deny me three times."[5] Entering Gethesemane, however, the press of what would shortly take place began to bear down on Jesus, which resulted in His being "sorrowful and troubled."[6] The weight of it all was very heavy. This would be the darkest night of His soul.

There among the olive trees, an oil press maybe even within sight, Jesus asked His eleven disciples to sit down and pray, but then He motioned Peter, James, and John to go farther into the garden with Him. Then He said, "My soul is exceedingly sorrowful, even to death. Stay here and watch with Me."[7] We're told He left the three there and went a stone's throw away from them, fell on His face, and prayed, "O My Father, if it is possible, let this cup pass from Me; nevertheless, not as I will, but as You will."[8] Jesus wasn't praying some nice homiletic prayer. He was groaning to the Father. *Though the disciples didn't know it at the time, Jesus was modeling for them how they needed to get ready for what was fast approaching. He was showing them not only their need for oil, but how to get oil: Watch with Him. Watch and pray.*

Jesus returned to where Peter, James, and John were sitting, and He found them asleep. Waking up Peter, Jesus said to him, "What! Could you not watch with Me one hour? Watch and pray, lest you enter into temptation. The spirit indeed is willing, but the flesh is weak."[9] Here was a personal correction and warning to Peter to get ready. Jesus wanted Peter to have the oil, the power, to not succumb to the temptation that would soon be crouching at Peter's door. But Peter couldn't stay awake. As much as Jesus wanted Peter, James, and John—His inner circle —to pray *with* Him, and we may even infer to pray *for* Him— Jesus wanted them to be alert and pray for what they were about to face. He had done all His due diligence in teaching them in the days before His agony in the garden. He had told them about the signs of His coming—how they were to be alert, watchful, and prayerful. He had told them repeatedly to watch. He had even given them the parable of the ten virgins, highlighting the fact that all ten had fallen asleep; however, five had trimmed the wicks of their lamps and had plenty of oil. *This was the disciples' opportunity to make themselves ready right along with Jesus as He was preparing Himself in the olive grove, probably near an olive press—everything was pointing in neon lights to their need of oil.* But as Luke's account tells us, Jesus "found them sleeping from sorrow."[10]

Not being there in the flesh with the disciples and Jesus, we can miss the very real heaviness the disciples felt at that hour. Their Master was saying things they never heard come out of His mouth before. "My soul is exceedingly sorrowful—even unto death." The way the disciples experienced the urgency of the hour was to come under the heaviness of it. It pressed them. It pressed Jesus. The atmosphere was heavy, perhaps crushing even. And the disciples' flesh succumbed to sleep. That's how the weight of it all affected them. We need to remember that before we become critical or harsh in our assessments of them, especially Peter. *The truth is their warning is our warning. Their difficulty is our difficulty. Their sleepiness only exposes our own.*

We know the rest of the story. How Jesus went to the disciples on three occasions, only to find them asleep each time. Then our Savior went to the press, and Luke tells us, "And being in agony, He prayed more earnestly. Then His sweat became like great drops of blood falling down to the ground."[11] After this, He woke up the disciples and then was soon arrested. What Jesus had told them when leaving the Upper Room happened: "You will all fall away because of me this night. For it is written, 'I will strike the shepherd, and the sheep of the flock will be scattered.'"[12] His disciples, His sheep, scattered.

RESPONDING TO THE CALL

Jesus wants us to watch just like He wanted His disciples to watch. And what He is saying to us is this, "I want you to be in this militant stance in your prayers with Me. Your intercession matters. Pray with Me. Buy oil and stay awake. Will you not watch with Me?"

I really believe Jesus wants us to understand—wants His Church to understand—that a dark night, a very difficult time, is coming. He is offering us, just as He did before His crucifixion, an opportunity to get prepared. He is waking us up and admonishing us to stay awake because being watchful and prayerful will help us get through the darkness of the hour and overcome temptation. *We as the Church will enter into a state of power and strength and partnership with Jesus, our great Intercessor, at the end of the age. And we will do that by watching with Him, praying with Him, and growing in intimacy and knowledge and revelation of Him. That's His plan for us.*

The exercises of watching and praying are exercises we do in the Holy Spirit so that we will not be overcome or dominated by the world, the flesh, or the devil. And *a vibrant secret place relationship with the Lord in the place of prayer and watchfulness will make us a real threat to hell.* That's why Jesus calls us to it, especially in these last days. If you, however, view or appraise the world through the lens of the flesh, through the lenses of the leaven we discussed in chapter eleven, you will become disoriented and fall prey to the destroyer. But if you view everything through the lens of the Spirit, then you can have victory. You can see and watch and react according to the Holy Spirit's intelligence and reconnaissance.

Beloved, we need to have a real expectancy like the early Church did. God is calling for watchmen to be set on the wall of intercession. Isaiah 62:6 talks about watchmen set on the walls of Jerusalem, who "all day and all the night they shall never be silent." These watchmen, according to the next verse, will "take no rest, and give [the Lord] no rest until he establishes Jerusalem and makes it a praise in the earth." *Part of our watchman call is to put God in remembrance of His promises over Israel and the city of Jerusalem. We also need to be praying for the Church to become mature and ready for the Lord's return.* We must respond to the high calling of God in this hour as intercessors who are watchful and prayerful.

I really believe that every single believer alive on the planet is called to be an intercessor—to be a watchman. You're called to be an intercessor. You're called to take your place on the wall. You're not called to hide out like Gideon did in your cave somewhere, waiting and trying to survive. You're called to enter into the secret place because, if you don't enter the secret place, you will enter into temptation. *I want to call you today, not to a place of fear, but to vigilance, watchfulness, and prayerfulness.* What would happen if you and I responded to Jesus' invitation to be overcoming intercessors and people who are watchful and prayerful in this hour? It would shift atmospheres and win our cities for God.

I believe you and I are called to be a part of a generation of intercessors, a fully mature Church in the end times, that is not defeated by darkness, that is not dominated by the spirit of antichrist, but is fully saturated by the Holy Spirit of God, walking in unity together, praying and shifting atmospheres and releasing revival upon those around us. If we respond to His call to the wall of intercession, to be faithful and prayerful in our watch, we will see millions of people come into the Kingdom of God and Jesus receive the rewards of His suffering.

_____

1. Romans 13:11.
2. Mark 13:9, 33, 34, 35, and 37.
3. The Greek *blepō* is used for Mark 13:33. The word *grēgoreō* is used for Mark 34, 35, 37. And *agrypneō* is used for Mark 13:33.
4. The recent discovery of a *Mikveh* in the Gethsemane area "confirms the ancient name of the place" as this would be where workers involved in oil making would have taken their ritual baths. Ylenia Granito, "Ancient Olive Oil Production Artifact Found in Gethsemane," Olive Oil Times, January 6, 2021, http://tinyurl.com/yc6acfmx/ (accessed January 23, 2024).
5. Matthew 26:34.
6. Matthew 26:37.
7. Matthew 26:38 NKJV.
8. Matthew 26:39 NKJV.
9. Matthew 26:40–41 NKJV.
10. Luke 22:45 NKJV.
11. Luke 22:44 NKJV.
12. Matthew 26:31–32.

THIRTEEN
PRAY: THE CALL TO ENGAGE IN FAITH & PREVAIL

A WATCHFUL ATTITUDE and a prayerful lifestyle at the end of the age are going to be the antidote to the virus of spiritual slumber. In Luke 21:36, Jesus admonished His disciples with these words, "But stay awake at all times, praying that you may have strength to escape all these things that are going to take place, and to stand before the Son of Man." What was Jesus saying? There is a prescription. *There is a way to live your life whereby you can prevail and overcome, living a life of victory, even during some of the hardest and darkest days of history.*

How do we get that strength? By staying awake and praying —by responding to the urgency of the hour with watchfulness and prayerfulness. We need to stand on our watchtowers— beholding what is happening on the horizon, looking through a Kingdom of God lens of faith rather than fear, not being weighed down with depression and anxiety—and looking for the return of our Lord Jesus. This kind of watching leads to prayer. And that prayer leads to escaping and overcoming.

HOW TO ESCAPE & OVERCOME

Throughout God's Word, we see the many times God was faithful to warn His leaders, His prophets, and His people of an impending judgment or disaster. I think of World War 2 and even modern-day military campaigns in which leaflets that inform people to evacuate the area because of an airstrike to come are airdropped. Of course, warnings today can be given via text or social media even. But the point is to give someone an opportunity to escape harm.

As we've discussed, Jesus was warning His disciples in the Olivet Discourse, giving them instructions on how to navigate through the coming days. He specifically told them what to pray as we saw in Luke 21:36, for example: Pray for strength to escape what's coming and strength to stand before Jesus. He told them to pray that certain events wouldn't happen in winter or on the Sabbath.[1] He exhorted them to pray so that they wouldn't succumb to temptation.[2] But there were other things that Jesus taught His disciples about prayer that should also be helpful to us in the darkest hour.

Jesus taught His disciples how to pray after they entreated Him. He said:

Pray then like this: "Our Father in heaven, hallowed be your name. Your kingdom come, your will be done, on earth as it is in heaven. Give us this day our daily bread, and forgive us our debts, as we also have forgiven our debtors. And lead us not into temptation, but deliver us from evil."

MATTHEW 6:9–13

He gave more instruction about how to pray in the parable of the persistent widow before the unjust judge, the point of which was to teach them "that they ought always to pray and not lose heart."[3]

Furthermore, Jesus said radical things like, "Whatever you ask in prayer, believe that you have received it, and it will be yours," or "Bless those who curse you, pray for those who abuse you," or "But I say to you who hear, Love your enemies, do good to those who hate you."[4]

And then there were those things that He prayed, modeling for us how we should pray—

- "Father, forgive them, for they know not what they do."[5]
- "Father, if you are willing, remove this cup from me. Nevertheless, not my will, but yours be done."[6]
- "Simon, Simon, behold, Satan demanded to have you, that he might sift you like wheat, but I have prayed for you that your faith may not fail. And when you have turned again, strengthen your brothers."[7]

Jesus' instructions teach us that prayer is essential always, and it will become even more essential as we confront the enemy in the darkness.

PRAYER: A TOOL OF THE WARRIOR

Those infrared, night vision goggles are what we need. They are a tool of a warrior. Navy Seals have really advanced ones, so you could drop the Seals into a zero-light environment, and they would put their goggles on and be able to see all around them. The infrared goggles enable them to see people, see any movement or action of the enemy, and navigate through the darkness. If you've ever been in a very dark room, you know it is only a matter of time before you run into something. Night vision helps a warrior see his enemy and know what's going on.

Jesus has given us spiritual night vision. It is called prayer. *Prayer enables the eyes of your spirit to be opened so that you can function in the middle of the darkness in the world.* You can navigate in prayer through the help of the Holy Spirit. You can even walk in and by the Spirit.[8] You can keep in step with the Holy Spirit all the way. I love how the apostle Paul spoke about "having the eyes of [our] hearts enlightened."[9] Paul told the believers in Ephesus that he was praying for them that God would open the eyes of their inner man—their spirit. He was talking about their receiving spiritual sight.

There is a way for us to live spiritually, to appraise what's happening through prayer and the lens of the Holy Spirit. The rest of the world is going to see things that happen in the natural, and they will view and interpret it according to the flesh, but if you and I will be people of prayer, we will be able to prevail. And the reason we will prevail is because we will have the strength to do so.

INTIMACY & PREVAILING PRAYER

Not all prayer is equal. Many often say, "Prayer changes things." No, it doesn't. *Prayer in the name of Jesus accompanied by faith changes things.* Prayer alone is simply words or thoughts even. But praying to God in the power of the Holy Spirit and believing God is able, He is willing, and He will answer is the kind of prayer that changes things. Prevailing prayer is what we will need to use in the final days of history to overcome.

Some people have a very devotional and meditative idea about prayer. And devotion and meditation are ways in which we can commune and fellowship with God. However, certain individuals may try to convince you that it is the only way to pray. They might say, "I go out into the woods and surround myself in nature—out among the trees and the wildlife—where I become one with nature. That's my sanctuary where I meditate. And that's prayer." No, that's not prayer. That person is taking a hike, but when you stand in faith by the grace of God in the name of Jesus and partner with the Holy Spirit in accordance with the Scriptures—when you ask as a child of God, believing God will give you what you ask because you're asking in His will—now, that's prayer. That prayer will change circumstances, it will change atmospheres, and it will change you.

Jesus told us prevailing prayer would help us navigate the age that we are living in. Prevailing prayer will require intimacy with Jesus. When describing His own prayer life, Jesus said:

> Truly, truly, I say to you, the Son can do nothing of his own accord, but only what he sees the Father doing. For whatever the Father does, that the Son does likewise. For the Father loves the Son and shows him all that he himself is doing. And greater works than these will he show him, so that you may marvel.
>
> JOHN 5:19–20

The Son of God, the second Member of the Trinity, who has all authority, said He couldn't do anything of His own accord. He could only do what He witnessed His Father doing. While Jesus was on the earth, He apparently could see what the Father was doing. How did Jesus see the Father? Jesus saw the Father through the eyes of the spirit of prayer. He got alone with the Father. He recognized that, in and of Himself, He could do nothing apart from what He saw His Father do.

In John 8:38, while speaking to the Pharisees, Jesus said, "I speak of what I have seen with my Father, and you do what you have heard from your father." Within a few verses, Jesus told them who their father was—the devil. He was letting the Pharisees know that *our actions, the way we live our lives, and the trajectory of our lives tell us who our father is.*

When Jesus was in the secret place of prayer, when He was not with His disciples, He got alone with the Father. You could go through your Bible and highlight every time it says that, long before daybreak, Jesus went to a deserted place, and He prayed. Sometimes, He would go up on a mountain and pray all night. Think about this. Jesus was and is God, yet He prayed. Why? Because His prayer life was about His relationship with the Father. It was about the intimacy He shared with the Father. Yet you and I aren't God, and we don't pray. We act as if we can handle life on our own and even walk in obedience without praying.

Basically, Jesus accused the Pharisees of spending all their time being educated by hell. Yet Jesus spent all His time getting His opinions, His identity, and His marching orders from being alone with the Father in prayer. That's intimacy. When there was nobody to preach to, when nobody was asking Him to multiply the bread and the fish, when nobody was pressing in and trying to grab the hem of His garment, what did we find Jesus doing? Getting alone with the Father.

I believe God the Father highlighted Scriptures to Jesus, gave Him impressions and desires, and Jesus understood those by the Spirit. He listened to the Father's voice and was able to hear it above the din of the disciples and the crowd. He would then walk in that intimate place of prayer with the Father and do ministry.

What would our lives look like if we spent the first portion of our day or the last portion of our day—or even multiple portions of our day—getting alone with the Father and putting on our night vision goggles of the prayer of faith? We would be encouraged, we would be strengthened, we would do what we saw our Father doing, we would say what He wants us to say, and we would be able to navigate the darkness when everybody else is stumbling and getting trapped by it. Having been with the Father, we would have night vision, and we would be able to navigate all the traps of the enemy and prevail.

PERSISTENCE & PREVAILING PRAYER

Prevailing prayer must be persistent. Once again, the parable of the widow with the unjust judge in Luke 18 shows us that *persistence in the right direction pays off.* We're challenged by the message to always pray and not lose heart. The very reason many drop out when it comes to developing a consistent prayer life, or they stop petitioning God in prayer, is because they lose heart.

Let me make something clear here. It is important to note that prayer is not a performance. *The Pharisees tried to impress people and God through their prayer performances, but persistent prayer comes from relationship.* Remember, prevailing prayer requires intimacy with God. The Father isn't withholding from us because we're not "doing" prayer right or "performing" prayer long enough. The issue even in the Garden of Gethsemane was an issue of intimacy and relationship. "Could you not pray with

Me for an hour?" wasn't Jesus' golden rule of prayer. No, Jesus understood the way the human heart was developed and the way it can be strengthened and prepared for hard and difficult days is through practicing the Presence of God. *The human heart needs the Presence of God for life and strength and sustenance.*

We don't experience defeat spiritually in our lives because God's withholding something from us. No, we walk in less than the victory that actually belongs to us because we lose heart, we get tired, or we don't see any progress or fruitfulness. We live in a microwave culture. What we want to be able to do is pray something, and in thirty seconds, we want to see the manifestation of our request right in front of us. We want an angel to swoop down and save the day. We want one-minute prayer to manifest in a Minute-Rice-like result. We want God to be a microwave, and what we don't understand is He is actually more like a crockpot—slow and low, slow and low.

Prayer takes time. Intimacy takes time. Do not lose heart. Be persistent in prayer because the Bible tells you so. First Thessalonians 5:17 says, "Pray without ceasing." Colossians 4:2 tells us, "Continue steadfastly in prayer, being watchful in it with thanksgiving." These Scriptures aren't God's way of telling us we need to do more or pray in a way to tickle His fancy. God is not fickle or variable or moody. No, He is wanting us to understand the beat of our hearts needs to be in rhythm with Him and His Kingdom so that, no matter what comes against us, we can prevail because we have prayed and walked in intimacy with Him, and we have been persistent in prayer. What will happen if we pray persistently is, when our emotions try to limit us, or the accuser hurls his accusations at us, something on the inside of our spirit will rise up and will resist and turn to God for His love, protection, and direction.

How many times have we been so close to seeing a miracle breakthrough, but yet we have lost heart? You want prayer that prevails? That will come out of an intimate prayer life with God. It will happen when you're persistent and don't lose heart.

MILITANCY & PREVAILING PRAYER

Prevailing prayer has to be militant. Look at Ephesians 6:18 one last time. After Paul commanded the Church to put on God's armor, he wrote, "Praying at all times in the Spirit, with all prayer and supplication. To that end, keep alert with all perseverance, making supplication for all the saints." Here's what I want to propose to you. *The whole context of Ephesians 6—of Paul speaking about the armor of God—is talking about prayer. It is all talking about prayer.* When you pray, you put on the helmet of salvation. When you pray, you put on the breastplate of righteousness, the belt of truth, etc. When you pray, it is like getting ready for combat. Can you see that with me?

We've spoken about the must-have military mindset, and we've also spoken about the weaponry we have. *We must begin to see ourselves as soldiers in God's army.* I can't stress this enough. We are living in a combat zone, and we can't afford to act like casual civilians. *We must be militant—praying always with all prayer, with all supplication, and in the power of the Holy Spirit.*

Soldier, I believe with all of my heart that, if we were able to pull back the curtain and see into the spirit realm and see with our Spirit vision, we would not evaluate each other according to the flesh. We would see the anointing in each other. We would recognize the value of the call and purposes of God in each other. If we were to take our night vision goggles and look at ourselves in the mirror, we would stop denigrating ourselves, stop letting the accuser slander us, and end his attempts to deconstruct us and bring us down. We would see that we are washed and that we are clothed in robes of royalty. We would watch the angels move at the sound of our weakest prayers and watch as the demons tremble.

We must believe that we can prevail even in the midst of the gross darkness. Jesus is coming back for a glorious Church—a victorious and overcoming Church—who has beheld His beauty in the secret place. He is returning for a Bride whose heart has been captivated by the Presence of God. But make no mistake, His Bride will be wearing armor, wielding the sword of the Word with great power, and she will be found ready and prevailing in prayer. God is building His Church—He is building us—into a people of prayer, a people of faith, a people of worship, and a people who will overcome.

---

1. See Matthew 24:20; Mark 13:18.
2. See Matthew 26:41; Mark 14:38; Luke 22:40, 46.
3. Luke 18:1.
4. Mark 11:24; Luke 6:27–28.
5. Luke 23:34.
6. Luke 22:42.
7. Luke 22:31–32.
8. See Galatians 5:16.
9. Ephesians 1:18.

FOURTEEN
OVERCOMING IN THE LAST DAYS

WHAT DO we know now about the last days? Well, we know there's going to be an increase of natural phenomena. There's going to be an increase of spiritual violence and lawlessness. We're seeing it all across the globe already. And then there will be betrayal. Neighbors, co-workers, family members, and complete strangers will betray one another, which means there's going to be persecution. In 2 Timothy 3:12, the apostle Paul told Timothy, "Indeed, all who desire to live a godly life in Christ Jesus will be persecuted." If you're going to love Jesus, you're not going to be popular. If you're going to live righteously in this generation, you're not going to be celebrated. You might be tolerated, but more than likely, you will be persecuted. You need to settle it right now in your heart that you will face difficult days.

Man, I'm not ready for that, you might think. This is your opportunity to prepare. Prepare yourself for the violence, the natural disasters, the hatred, the persecution, the lawlessness, and the violence. Ready yourself for the return of the Lord. *The great shaking has already begun, and the best way through what's ahead is to pursue the great love of your heart, the One to whom you're betrothed—Jesus. Get to know Him. Grow in your intimacy. Buy oil.* Be ready to participate in the greatest ingathering of souls and the proclamation of the gospel to all ethnic groups around the world. Let your heart be set aflame with love for Jesus in the face of difficult days, amid a culture that thinks you're crazy.

Beloved, we're going to take the love of Jesus and His message to the north. We're going to take it to the south. We're going to take it to the east and the west. We're going to Asia, Europe, South America, and Africa. We're going to Central America. We're going to Australia. We might even preach to the penguins in Antarctica. But we will take this gospel to all the nations of the world, the whole world. That's what we will do.

I want you to imagine millions of believers encountering the Presence of the Lord when the rest of the world is faltering, getting offended, hating, murdering, and turning on each other. Right in the middle of that, God's going to raise up strong, bold, courageous people who have been formed in the forge of the fires of persecution. That's who we're called to be. *Man will not be able to bend or break us because we have gazed upon the One who sits upon the throne, and we preach with boldness and courage, moving in signs and wonders.* That's when we'll be fully deployed, engaged, and mobilized at the coming of the Lord.

We want to be one of those bold witnesses who's found faithful. We want our intimacy, prayer, and worship to propel us to partner with our coming King to fulfill the mission. We want to be wide awake. We want to take heed to ourselves. We want to watch. We want to pray. We want to stand at attention and see the salvation of our Lord with our own eyes. Let's determine in our hearts today to be a part of what God is doing in the earth. Together, let's take heed, watch, and pray!

A PRAYER OF RESPONSE

Father, we are Your people, and, oh, how we want You to come in glory and power. Lord, we've heard of Your great power, we've heard all the accounts of how You've moved throughout the generations, we know how You've intervened in history, and we know that You are Sovereign and holy. In response to Your kindness, we ask that You would grant us repentance for not staying watchful, for not staying awake. Forgive us, Lord, for wanting to hide in the caves of culture. Wash us, cleanse us, and lead us out of the caves. We respond to Your call to prepare the way for what You're doing in the earth now and, ultimately, for Your return. Renew a right spirit in us, Your people. Renew our minds and calibrate our hearts to Your Kingdom's time zone. Awaken our hearts. Shake us out of our lethargy and dullness.

Lord, we as members of Your Body, the Church, we pray for the Church worldwide. Make us into that glorious Church You have created us to be. Remove the spots and steam out the wrinkles. We pray for those who are being persecuted or facing death for Your name's sake. Grant them courage and strength to face what's before them. Presence Yourself with them. May they see You standing as Stephen saw You when he was being stoned to death for his love and service to You.

Father, we pray for the peace of Jerusalem. Save Your covenant people. Remove the hardness from their hearts and take away the veil from their eyes so that they would see and know Jesus as their Messiah. Help us to love them and be faithful in prayer until You make Jerusalem a praise in all the earth. Send revival to Your land.

Father, we don't want to resist You or what You're doing in this hour. May we be humble before You and submit to what You need to do on the threshing floor of Your Church. May we be ready and awake, our lamps full of the oil of intimacy, for the hour that is coming, for the great and awful day of the Lord. We know difficult as well as glorious days are coming. May we respond in radical obedience to Your voice, calling us to be who You have called us to be. Soften our hearts again. Give us pliable hearts to respond to You. Revive first love for You in our hearts, and empower us to do the works of that love.

Lastly, we ask that You would help us prepare the way for Your coming—that we would be good soldiers, alert and awake as You have commanded us. Help us to take heed, watch, and pray. We look forward to Your return. Maranatha![1] *Lord Jesus, come.*

---

1. See 1 Corinthians 16:22 NASB.

ACKNOWLEDGMENTS

I want to take a moment and acknowledge the team that has been vital to the process of getting this message out. I am reminded of the model the apostle Paul gave us of the importance of team ministry. Even though we rightly acknowledge and honor Paul for his supernatural accomplishments, it is clear from his own benedictions that he knew how important the other members of his apostolic team were to the mission. In that spirit, I want to honor the members of my team that help me write books and get the message out that God has entrusted to me.

I want to thank Edie Mourey. The way you capture my voice, research all my messages, and help shape these books with the help of the Holy Spirit is a true gift.

Krista Kennedy, my executive assistant for many years, you help me organize my life, time, and project priority. I could not do all that I do without your help. Thank you.

Rick Burmeister, my right-hand man, you have said many times that your job description is "to bring the vision God gives me into reality." I am eternally grateful that God led you to leave behind the success of the corporate world to help me make an eternal difference.

Sean Downs is a profound gift to Radiant and the Kingdom of God. Your multifaceted gift mix has accelerated all that God has called me to do, and I appreciate you beyond what words can communicate.

Our creative team is made up of some of the most committed, creative, and forward-thinking individuals that I have ever worked with. Thank you for working with excellence.

Finally, I want to acknowledge the person that is my wife, friend, ministry partner, and everything else that words cannot describe. Jane, I would not be who I am today without the touch of God and the wife of my youth. I love you beyond words, and I am more confident today than I have ever been that two are better than one.

ABOUT THE AUTHOR

Lee Cummings is the founding and senior leader of Radiant Church. Lee and his wife, Jane, started Radiant in 1996 in a high school auditorium in Richland, Michigan, a rural community in the outskirts of Kalamazoo. Since then, Radiant Church has grown to reach thousands of people in several locations. Radiant is a praying and worshiping church that is relentlessly leading people to become fully formed disciples of Jesus Christ living on mission together.

Since 2016, Lee has also served as the founder and overseer of the Radiant Network, a family of churches and leaders who share a common vision for growing the Kingdom.

Lee and Jane currently reside in Kalamazoo. They were married in 1992 and have three grown children, two sons-in-law, and three grandchildren.

ALSO BY LEE CUMMINGS

An Overview of Why Israel Matters

Give No Rest! A Renewed Commitment to Pursue God's Presence in Prayer and Worship in the American Church

School of the Spirit: Living the Holy Spirit-Empowered Life

Be Radiant: Becoming Who God Meant You to Be

Flourish: Planting Your Life Where God Designed It to Thrive

SCAN FOR BOOKS, COURSES,
BLOGS, PODCASTS, AND MORE

@LEEMCUMMINGS

www.ingramcontent.com/pod-product-compliance
Lightning Source LLC
Chambersburg PA
CBHW020255130626

46549CB00005B/2226